# *iSpeak* to the *Earth:*

## Release Prosperity

**Rediscovering an Ancient Spiritual Technology for Manifesting Prosperity & Healing the Land!**

By

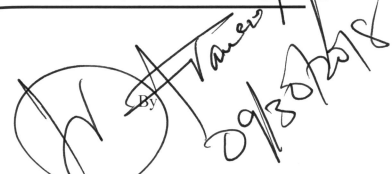

# DR. FRANCIS MYLES

*Includes Prayer of Activation!*

Published by
Francis Myles International  (in partnership with)
Dr. Francis Myles
P.O Box 2467
Scottsdale, Arizona 85252
www.FrancisMyles.com

For Worldwide Distribution Printed in the United States by Createspace (An Amazon Company)

# ACKNOWLEDGMENTS

*The Lord gave the word: great was the company of those that published it" (Psalm 68:11 KJV).*

WHAT WE BECOME IN GOD is a sum total of the divine encounters we have had, the people we have met, our personal experiences and the books we have read. The saying "No man is an island" is certainly true in the context of authoring this book. I want to acknowledge the impact that the following men and women of God have had on my life: Pastor Carmela Myles (my wife), His Majesty King Admatey I (Dr. Kingsley Fletcher), Dr. Jonathan David, Apostle Harrison Chileshe (my first pastor), Apostle John Eckhardt (who introduced me to the apostolic), Dr. John P. Kelly (who commissioned me as an apostle), Pastor Tom Deuschle, Dr. Gordon E. Bradshaw (my covenant brother and spiritual covering), Bishop Tudor Bismarck (for your friendship and being an exemplary global ambassador for the continent of Africa), Prophet Gershom Sikaala, Dr. Myles Munroe (I will never forget the last thing you told me before you transitioned to heaven)—their teachings and personal conversations with me over the years have added to the richness of this book.

While the material in this book is original, there are a few quotes throughout that have been taken from the published works of other notable Christian authors, which add depth to the topic or focus. Each is documented in the "Endnote Section."

# TABLE OF CONTENTS

# ENDORSEMENTS

Speaking to the Earth is a message that is very close to my heart. It is the costliest revelation that my husband, Dr. Francis Myles has ever experienced. I almost lost him two years ago but that experience produced a revelation that will forever change the nation of Zimbabwe. What the enemy meant for evil two years ago in Africa, the Lord used to save many lives in the same continent! I was with my husband in the nation of Zimbabwe when he released the message on "Speaking to the Earth" at Celebration Church in Borrowdale, Zimbabwe. What happened next is unprecedented. The Holy Spirit brooded over the darkness that has been hovering over this nation for over 37 years, the power of intercession from over 2,000 united people came forth and Dr. Myles prophesied and declared, "the land is now at rest, the earth beneath your feet has shifted!" Two weeks later, President Robert Mugabe was overthrown in a rare bloodless coup. Only God could have done this! I encourage you to read this life-changing book. Learn how to speak to the earth and let the earth release your inheritance!

**Carmela Real Myles**

*Co-Pastor, Lovefest Church International*

*Tempe, Arizona*

Once I read the first chapter, I was on the edge of my seat wanting to know how to do it! Well, Doctor Myles taught me exactly how. He leads you through a Bible-based teaching and then through an activation that will cause things in your life to dramatically SHIFT. Get ready for a breakthrough!

**Katie Souza**

*Expected End Ministries*

*Host of "Healing Soul Keys to the Miraculous" TV Show*

*Maricopa, Arizona*


Dr. Francis Myles has shown us that by receiving the word of the LORD in the heart and speaking that revelation out of the mouth in the power of the SPIRIT releases the ability of the FATHER to prosper us! As a child of GOD develops a relationship with the FATHER through the LORD JESUS, the power to exercise dominion is manifested and God's original intent for man to rule is evident. Doctor MYLES has taught us how to take authority over evil and reclaim what is ours! In this book you will discover how to overcome every obstacle , remove every hindrance, and bring heaven into the earth in the NAME OF JESUS. Speak to the earth and see the GLORY OF GOD!!

**Pastor Tony Kemp**

*Founder of the ACTS GROUP,*

*The Apostolic Council Teaching Services*

*Overseer and leader of Tony Kemp Ministries*

*Hannibal, Missouri*

The revelation of "Speaking to the Earth" is thunder from the throne room of God - thunder that will transform the land under your feet and revolutionize cities, states, and the nations of the world. Finally, a lost mystery of God is being restored to the Body of Christ that will redeem and heal the land! Prepare to see tangible results on a massive scale! A must read!

**Pastors Rob & Kay Winters**

*Prepare the Way International Church*

*Phoenix, AZ*

# FOREWORD

**M**any years ago, I was faced with the reality of the supernatural. Though I was a sincere believer and placed my faith and trust in God, I was unaware of the veracity of spiritual warfare that surrounds the believer. To this reality, I received a rude awakening at a summation point. One night while lying in my bed, I felt a strange demonic presence coming towards me, which began to suffocate me. The more I attempted to cry for help, the more this dark force muffled me in my room.

Finally, I screamed the words "Jesus!" It was then that I realized two things:

1. I realized the unseen realm was real.

2. I realized that the name of Jesus was greater than the darkness!

Since that time, I have been on an epic journey to help liberate God's people from the powers of darkness. In this epic book, *I Speak To The Earth*, my friend Dr. Francis Myles, imparts kingdom keys that will empower the believer to live the life God has always intended. As one who has traveled the globe, I have seen the devastation of witchcraft and the poverty and destitution it brings. We were created to have dominion in the Earth but unfortunately those who operate in the realm of darkness have more understanding of this truth than most believers.

It is time for us to take our place. It is time to speak to the Earth and command the Earth to yield its fruit to us. And it is time to exercise spiritual authority over witchcraft attacks from the evil one. This is a powerful tool in equipping the believer to reclaim what is rightfully theirs.

**Dr. Kynan Bridges**

Bestselling Author of Unmasking The Accuser and The Power of Prophetic Prayer.

Senior Pastor, Grace & Peace Global Fellowship Church, Tampa, FL

Founder, International Apostolic and Prophetic Council

www.graceempowered.org

# PREFACE

**T**HERE IS NOTHING more potent and life changing than revelation that is inspired by the Holy Spirit. Without revelation, we are left to dig through man's distorted view of reality, which we affectionately call the "information age." Unfortunately, information is a product of fallen man while God is the only One who produces the product called revelation. The advent of the Internet, Google, Yahoo and Bing search engines and the rise of social media platforms like Facebook and Twitter has led to the mass proliferation of information. Yet man's spiritual condition, for the most part, has only grown worse. Even with the mass proliferation of information, most humans are very ignorant as to their true purpose, worth and inherent God-given potential. Man's ignorance of his purpose inevitably causes him to misunderstand the purpose of the created order around him.

Once upon a time, eons ago, long before there was "anything," God existed only as Himself! In a God moment, He decided to create a special, life-sustaining planet called Earth. In the beginning God created the heavens and the Earth (Genesis 1:1), marks the beginning of the most important book in the Bible. Central to the divine intent for creating this special planet was God's "Big Idea" to create spirit children housed in bodies of dirt (Earth) that can dominate and subdue the Earth on behalf of the Kingdom of Heaven. As a consequence, the

Earth becomes a nursery of sorts for God's children and a sandbox for exercising man's God-given dominion. When God finally creates the first human, Adam, He established a very special relationship between Adam and the planet itself.

> *And God said, Let us make man in our image, after our likeness: and let them have dominion over the fish of the sea, and over the fowl of the air, and over the cattle, and over all the earth, and over every creeping thing that creepeth upon the earth. (Genesis 1:26)*

The greatest discovery in life is the discovery of purpose. The genesis of God's purpose for creating the human race can be found in the first two chapters of Genesis. From the beginning, our physical world (Earth) was designed to be a spiritual colony of the Kingdom of Heaven. According to Genesis 1:26, God gave Adam five areas of "dominion." We will quickly examine these five areas of dominion.

1. Dominion over the Marine kingdom (over the fish of the sea);
2. Dominion over the Bird kingdom (over the fowl of the air);
3. Dominion over the Animal kingdom (over the cattle);
4. Dominion over the Earth (The Earth's soil, solar system and all its natural resources);
5. Dominion over the Reptilian kingdom (over every creeping thing).

While the relationship God wanted to establish between man and the Earth is clearly one of absolute dominion, the fall of man inserted a wrinkle in that relationship. When Adam and Eve fell from dominion by violating a direct instruction from God, all of creation, including the Earth itself, fell with them. Since then, the Earth and its vast resources does not easily bring itself under man's delegated authority.

Most importantly, when Adam and Eve fell from grace, the ground beneath their feet began to give birth to thorns and thistles. "Thorns and thistles" are a prophetic picture of a curse. It is not easy trying to work a field full of thorns and thistles. This is why I highly recommend the subject of this book, *"Speaking to the Earth"* in order to cause it to bring forth! We must take authority over the Earth beneath our feet and command it to give us of its bounty. *In this book, you will discover an ancient spiritual technology for "speaking to the Earth in order to cause it to bring forth prosperity!"*

Yours for Kingdom Advancement

**Dr. Francis Myles**

Author of Bestseller: *The Order of Melchizedek*

Senior Pastor:Lovefest Church International, Arizona

Chancellor: The Order of Melchizedek Supernatural School of Ministry (francismyles.org)

Founder: Francis Myles International  (Francismyles.com)

# 1

# Contending with Witchcraft in Africa

*Surely there is no enchantment against Jacob, neither is theremany divination against Israel: according to this time it shall be said of Jacob and of Israel, What hath God wrought! (Numbers 23:23)*

O N MAY 17TH 2015, my dear and precious mother, Esther, died in the Republic of Zambia. Zambia is a peaceful and economically vibrant, land-locked country in Central Africa that gained its independence from Britain in 1964 under the leadership of a freedom fighter by the name of Kenneth Kaunda. By divine design, I was born and raised in this country. I also gave my life to Christ in this nation at the Maranatha Assemblies of God in a Metropolitan city called Kitwe, before I migrated to South Africa in 1994. Four years later, after functioning successfully as a healing evangelist in the rainbow nation of South Africa, I made my final migration to the United States of America under a special divine and apostolic commission from the Holy Spirit. I have had a fantastic time in ministry since migrating to the United States of America.

On May 17th, 2015, I received a text on my phone about my mother's death moments before I was scheduled to preach to a congregation under my spiritual covering in the state of North Carolina. I quickly excused myself. I went outside into the church's parking lot and wept. While tears flooded my eyes, I had a prophetic vision in which I saw my mother with her hands raised in worship entering the pearly gates of our precious Lord's heavenly city. I knew then without a shadow of doubt that my precious mother had crossed over into the arms of the Lord Jesus Christ. She was safely home! God's supernatural peace came over me like a warm blanket on a cold night. I wiped my eyes and went back into the church and preached one of my best sermons. The following day, I bought an air ticket and flew to Africa to attend my mother's funeral. Many people who had been touched by my mother's generosity and godly lifestyle showed up at her home-going celebration. Together, we gave my mother a glorious send off and put her body to rest.

## ZIMBABWE

On May 25th 2015, I was scheduled to fly out of Zambia to Zimbabwe to speak to over 5,000 delegates at Pastor Tom Deuschle's Action Conference in the nation's capital of Harare. On my way to the Kenneth Kaunda International Airport, I suddenly fell ill. I went from feeling fantastic to becoming deathly sick within a couple of minutes. It was the strangest demonic attack on my body I have ever experienced. I told Apostle Harrison (a leading pastor in Zambia) who was driving me to the airport at the time, *"I am feeling like I am being buried alive. Please pray for and with me."*

Suddenly, my blood pressure became dangerously high and physical exhaustion swept over my body like a tsunami. By the time we got to the airport in the outskirts of Lusaka (the capital city of Zambia), I could hardly walk. I got out of the car but not before I told the man of God who was driving me to stay in the airport parking lot until I confirmed to him that I was safely aboard the plane. I was quickly cleared through security and immigration check points but the closer I got to the Kenyan airways airplane, the weaker I became and my breathing became more labored.

I was feeling like I was being buried alive.

## IF YOU GET ON THE PLANE, YOU WILL DIE!

Even though it was now apparent even to me that I was very sick, what the Holy Spirit told me as I was walking towards the Kenyan airways plane brought me to an abrupt halt: *"Francis, if you get on the plane you will die!"* The voice of the Holy Spirit was gentle but very authoritative. I had no doubt in my mind that if I violated the warning of the Holy Spirit, I would die before I got to Zimbabwe. I called one of the airport security officers and told him to call for an ambulance. I knew that I was in serious warfare for my very life. I was rushed to an emergency clinic at the airport. I was given strong medication in an effort to lower my overly high blood pressure. Instead of the drugs lowering my blood pressure as expected, my blood pressure became worse to the amazement of the nurse on duty. The Lord told me not to focus on the high blood pressure but to realize that I was fighting against a very powerful witchcraft spell that had been released against my physical body. God did not want me to lose sight of the fact that I was in the middle of high-level spiritual warfare against demons.

*For we do not wrestle against flesh and blood, but against principalities, against powers, against the rulers of the darkness of this age, against spiritual hosts of wickedness in the heavenly places. Therefore take up the whole armor of God, that you may be able to withstand in the evil day, and having done all, to stand. Ephesians 6:12-13*

Hours later, emergency medical personnel at the airport clinic managed to lower my blood pressure sufficiently enough to rush me to a more sophisticated hospital, midtown. When I arrived at the St. Johns Medical Center, my uncle, Dr. Dan Pule (founder of TBN Zambia) and a few of my blood brothers, were waiting for my arrival anxiously. They had heard that I was very sick. Since my mother had just died, everyone was extremely concerned for my well-being. No one was looking forward to another funeral, especially one involving a first-born son. I told one of my brothers, Emmanuel, to mobilize intercessors in Zambia and the USA to pray tenaciously for my deliverance. The female doctor on duty at the hospital began to administer new medication to lower my alarmingly high blood pressure *but the feeling that I was dying and being buried alive never diminished.* I have never felt as close to death as I did then. I could smell the presence of the angel of death.

## FIGHTING FOR MY LIFE

I was admitted at the St. Johns Medical hospital so they could observe me overnight. I knew in my spirit that I was in for a very rough night. My younger brother, Stephen, volunteered to stay the night with me to tend to my needs. I was so weak I could hardly get up to go to the restroom. Just a few minutes past midnight, my wife (who had stayed behind in America) and a dear friend of mine, Prophet Gershom Sikaala, called me on a 3-way phone call from the United States of America. Before I could say anything, he proceeded to prophesy; *"Man of God, your body is not really sick. You are fighting high-level witchcraft that has been released against you. The Lord showed me that one of the women who came to your mother's funeral is part of the group of witches that are assigned to kill you. They have said that your body will not leave Zambia alive!"*

My friend, my wife and I began to pray profusely against the spirit of witchcraft after he finished prophesying. We prayed together for about forty minutes before Prophet Gershom declared boldly, *"The yoke of witchcraft is broken, man of God! You will not die in Zambia. You are coming home to America!"* As soon as he said this, I felt a tangible spiritual weight lift off my physical body. Physical strength began to return to my body almost immediately. I got off the phone and stood up from my hospital bed. However the physical sensation of feeling like half of my body was being buried alive in dirt never subsided. So I knew my deliverance was not yet complete!

## "SON, SPEAK TO THE EARTH!"

*Give ear, O ye heavens, and I will speak; and hear, O earth, the words of my mouth. (Deuteronomy 32:1)*

*"Get up and go outside!"* Once again the voice of the Holy Spirit thundered in my spirit man. I told my baffled young brother to take me outside into the hospital yard. It was between 1 and 2 AM in the wee hours of the morning. I had no idea as to why the Lord wanted me to go outside but I knew I would soon find out. I have proven it several times over in my life, "obedience is better than sacrifice." Outside in the hospital yard, the night sky was brightened only by isolated stars and a half-crescent moon. I was thankful for the hospital security lights that added to the night's visibility.

*"Go to the flower bed!"* The Holy Spirit declared. I walked over to the flowerbed near the wall that surrounded the hospital. *"Son, take soil from the ground and speak to it. The people who want to kill you have instructed the soil of Zambia to swallow your body. You need to reverse this demonic instruction over the soil; your voice has preeminence over those who are trying to kill you because you are the redeemed of the Lord. The spell of witchcraft that was released on the soil is the pull you are feeling on your mortal body."* Even though I had never done anything like this before, I did not hesitate in my obedience. I quickly dipped my hand and pulled some soil from the ground beneath my feet.

I found myself under the inspiration of the Holy Spirit prophesying, these words: *"Earth, Earth hear the Word of the Lord. O soil of Zambia, you will not have my body in Jesus' name. O Earth, I release you from every evil instruction that these witches gave you to work against me in Jesus' mighty name, I pray. I am an apostle of Jesus*

17

Christ to the United States of America so I must return to America in Jesus' name. O Earth, I now ask you to open your mouth and swallow all the witchcraft that has been released against me in Jesus' mighty name." As soon as I finished praying, prophesying and making these decrees, the strangest thing happened. The downward pull that I had been experiencing in my legs disappeared instantly. *I knew in that instant that I would live and not die.*

"*Now put back the soil in your hand into the Earth beneath and I will bury those who tried to bury you,*" The Spirit of God declared authoritatively. When I placed the soil back in the dirt, something supernatural happened! I experienced a sudden infusion of life and supernatural energy. This surge of energy coursed through my physical body from the toes on my feet to the top of my head. I knew instantly that I would be discharged from the hospital the following morning, no matter what! I walked back to my hospital room feeling fantastic!

*However, once I was back in my hospital room, the theologian inside of me went into deep theological contemplation.* I said to the Lord, "*What was that?*" I wanted the Lord to give me a clear and sound doctrinal basis for what He had just led me to do. The truth be told, *I love the Word of God more than I love prophetic and supernatural experiences.* It's simply the way the LORD has wired me. I knew by how well I was feeling in my physical body that the *prophetic act of speaking to the Earth had actually saved my life.* But "why?" Why the good Lord chose this particular method to *deliver me from impending death* became the million-dollar question in my theologically inquisitive mind. I had to know because according to Deuteronomy 29:29, the "things" that are revealed to us by God are for our benefit and the benefit of our children's children.

## OUT OF THE DUST BACK TO THE DUST!

*In the sweat of thy face shalt thou eat bread, till thou return unto the ground; for out of it wast thou taken: for dust thou art, and unto dust shalt thou return. (Genesis 3:19)*

I have learned over the years of walking with God that if I don't fully understand something the Holy Spirit is doing, He will faithfully guide me into all truth. Jesus promised us that His Spirit would guide us into all truth (John 16). When I asked the Holy Spirit to explain to me why the spell of the witches of Africa spoken over the dust of the ground could affect my physical body in such a dreadful way, the Holy Spirit's response was swift and amazingly scriptural. By the time the Holy Spirit finished explaining, I was dazzled and beautifully inspired. I was also reminded of the Scripture in the book of Hosea that says, "My people are destroyed for the lack of knowledge (Hosea 4:6)." So I will now try to rephrase what the Holy Spirit told me. However, it will take this entire book to download and unpack this powerful revelation. This revelation is the equivalent of releasing a nuclear bomb in the natural! It's truly a spiritual nuclear arsenal.

"Son, take soil from the ground and speak to it. The people who want to kill you have instructed the soil of Zambia to swallow your body."

The Holy Spirit said to me, *"Francis, you were created with a body of dust that houses your spirit man. Since you have a body of dust that originates from the Earth, any demonically empowered witchcraft spell spoken over the dust against you can have a drastic impact on your well-being unless you (as the redeemed of the Lord) give the Earth (the dust beneath) a higher and righteous instruction than the one it's been told to obey by the children of wickedness."*

I was stunned by the Holy Spirit's answer. I instantly became hungrier for more revelation on this unfolding subject. I was not disappointed. The Holy Spirit gave me more scriptures to explain what I had just experienced. This experience is what precipitated the writing of the book you are now holding in your hands. The revelation contained in this book was also part of the spiritual arsenal the Lord used to supernaturally shift and begin to heal the nation of Zimbabwe, by abruptly ending 37 years of dictatorial rule by Robert Mugabe (more on this in Chapter Ten). At the end of this book, I have included a prayer of activation to teach you how to speak to the Earth to cause it to release prosperity or thwart the diabolical plans of the enemy against your God-given destiny and Kingdom assignment! The "Speaking to the Earth Prayer" also includes apostolic and prophetic decrees you can use to release the land from its "iniquity" so righteousness can reign in your country or geographical region. God wants to heal the land beneath our feet, which is in convulsions because of the iniquity placed upon it by our personal and national sin. Not to mention the wicked actions of our forefathers from previous generations. "For the land is defiled; therefore I visit the punishment of its iniquity upon it, and the land vomits out its inhabitants. You shall therefore keep My statutes and My judgments, and shall not commit any of these abominations, either any of your own nation or any stranger who dwells among you (for all these abominations the men of the land have done, who were before you, and thus the land is defiled), (Leviticus 18:25-27)." *Are you ready to learn everything the Holy Spirit showed me in the Word about how to animate this ancient spiritual technology for manifesting dominion and releasing prosperity here on Earth?* I bet you are! Let us plow ahead. The Earth beneath your feet is about to shift significantly!

# LIFE APPLICATION SECTION
# MEMORY VERSES

*"For the land is defiled; therefore I visit the punishment of its iniquity upon it, and the land vomits out its inhabitants. 26 You shall therefore keep My statutes and My judgments, and shall not commit any of these abominations, either any of your own nation or any stranger who dwells among you 27 (for all these abominations the men of the land have done, who were before you, and thus the land is defiled)."* Leviticus 18:25-27

# REFLECTIONS

1. Who is the first being in the Bible to speak to the Earth?

_____

_____

_____

_____

_____

2. Can the land be defiled?

_____

_____

_____

_____

_____

# 2

# Earth: A Divine Resource Center

*"You alone are the Lord. You made the skies and the heavens and all the stars. You made the earth and the seas and everything in them. You preserve them all, and the angels of heaven worship you." (Nehemiah 9:6 NLT)*

THE FIRST THING the Holy Spirit told me is that *everything God does He does it from a position of foreknowledge.* God's foreknowledge is the reason He is God and we are not! God's foreknowledge is His intrinsic and flawless ability to know the end from the beginning. This is why God never begins anything on Earth unless it's already finished in Heaven. God creates and fashions everything in the created universe from this same vantage point. Consider the following Scripture:

*Declaring the end from the beginning, and from ancient times things that are not yet done, Saying, 'My counsel shall stand, and I will do all My pleasure,'(Isaiah 46:10)*

The above passage of Scripture from the mouth of the Prophet Isaiah clearly establishes the immutability of God's foreknowledge, *"declaring the end from the beginning concerning the "things" not yet done "here on Earth."* What a wonderful statement about our God from the holy writ! Even the life, suffering, death and resurrection of the Lord Jesus Christ were never left to chance as the Scripture below clearly indicates.

*All who dwell on the earth will worship him, whose names have not been written in the Book of Life of the Lamb slain from the foundation of the world. (Revelation 13:8)*

The Holy Spirit showed me that "Earth" is also a very special product of God's foreknowledge and His unfathomable love for mankind who are the legal residents of this beautiful planet. Modern scientists and ancient astrologers have been dazzled by the amazing complexities of our universe and the multiple galaxies inside it. The invention of the telescope just fueled more questions and theories about our planetary system. What certainly baffles many members of the scientific community is the knowledge that the Earth we live on is one of the smallest planets in the solar system. Nevertheless, it is the only planet thus far in all of man's outer space explorations that has been proven to support life. Why? I believe God leaves us breadcrumbs of complexities that are designed to help us look for an intelligent designer behind the complex but orderly systems that support life on Earth.

Students of the Bible, on the other hand, do not share the same level of perplexity about the Earth, as does the scientific community because the Bible is full of scriptures that demonstrate why our small planet is the only one capable of sustaining human life. The first chapter in the book of Genesis is very clear as to the origins of our species and the planet we live on. Planet Earth, arguably one of the smallest planets in our solar system, is the "nursery" God chose for His spirit children encased in houses of dirt (humus). Consequently, God blessed the Earth with everything needed to sustain life. Simply said, planet Earth is full of divinely endowed resources needed to sustain life for billions of life forms that live on Earth until the end of this dispensation of time. This fact flies in the face of those who believe that the Earth's resources are diminishing rapidly.

# #1. THE EARTH IS THE LORD'S

*The **earth** is the Lord's, and the fullness thereof; the world, and they that dwell therein. (Psalm 24:1)*

The above passage of Scripture is loaded with "keys" for understanding Earth's uniqueness. We will breakdown this scripture systematically so we can mine it for precious nuggets of truth concerning the planet we live on.

Firstly, the expression *"the Earth is the Lord's,"* suggests that God retains total ownership of the planet Earth. God retains full ownership rights of the planet Earth primarily because He created it from nothing. The Earth is a product of God's eternal genius. The expression *"the Earth is the Lord's,"* also suggests that there is no single human who knows everything God embedded inside the belly of the Earth and what it's capable of. The One who created the Earth is the only Being who knows what she (Earth) is capable of doing and becoming. It's very presumptuous of us (humans) to think that we know what the Earth is capable of from our limited knowledge of the Earth's geology and topography. Whatever we know about the Earth will continue to evolve because there is more to our life-sustaining planet than we know currently. Additionally, the planet we live on was created by a God who is essentially a Spirit being (John 4:23). It, therefore, follows that there is a spiritual dimension to the planet Earth that can never be discerned with the naked eye. Appreciating this aspect of the Earth's inherent potential and purpose requires a revelation from God. It's a sure sign of great humility on our part to look to scripture to try to understand the planet Earth and our very unique relationship to it.

The Holy Spirit told me that everything God does He does it from a position of foreknowledge.

## #2. THE EARTH'S FULLNESS

*The **earth** is the Lord's, and the fullness thereof; the world, and they that dwell therein. (Psalm 24:1)*

The second key to understanding the invisible spirit dynamics of this wonderful planet we live on is centered on the expression, ***"and the fullness thereof."*** For the longest time, whenever I read this scripture, I completely missed the preciousness of this expression in the sacred text. I thought it was referring to the billions of people who live on this precious planet we all share. However, the Holy Spirit showed me that the expression *"and they that dwell therein;"* is the one that refers to the billions of people who live on this planet. This means then that the expression ***"and the fullness thereof"*** must be referencing something "else" specific to the Earth and different from the multitudes of people who live on Earth.

Suddenly, under divine inspiration, I saw it! *It was like turning on a light bulb.* The Holy Spirit showed me that the expression *"and the fullness thereof"* is referring to all the natural, scientific, chemical, technical and mineral resources that God, in His eternal providence, embedded in the belly of the Earth. The Holy Spirit said to me, "Francis, the belief that there exists <u>lack</u>, *any kind of lack,* on planet Earth is *the greatest lie from the enemy that my people have ever believed!"* This statement stunned me. The Holy Spirit showed me that when God created the Earth, He filled its belly or womb with every visible and invisible resource that mankind would ever need to satisfy God's demand upon our life until the day we die. "Why would God create the Earth and not fill it with every resource that we would ever need to fulfill our God given destiny in the Kingdom of heaven?" The Holy Spirit allowed His question to linger in my inquisitive mind.

The Holy Spirit showed me that airplanes existed in the womb of the Earth centuries before the Wright brothers came up with the idea of creating machinery that can fly. All the raw materials that would be needed for mankind to create a machine that can fly for hours in the sky were already deposited by God Himself in the belly of the Earth long before men dreamed of flying. Interestingly enough, even the idea and desire to want to fly was birthed inside the spirit of man by divine inspiration. Have you ever examined the inside and outside of a plane? You will quickly discover that there is nothing that went into building a plane, which did not ultimately come from manipulating natural, chemical or mineral resources that were already lying dormant in the Earth beneath our feet or around us.

The Holy Spirit showed me that even the cell phone that I use as my mobile office did not originate from heaven. Apart from the "idea" behind the creation of cell phone technology, all the raw materials to actually manufacture the device and make it usable came from the Earth beneath. Imagine this: for thousands of years our ancestors were traveling thousands of miles, days on end, on primitive creatures such as donkeys. All the while, the Lord knew that millions of automobiles were trapped in the womb of the Earth, waiting for mankind to get a revelation (idea) from God on how to manipulate the Earth's unlimited resources to produce these wonderful machines. Fortunately for us, the mantle for this assignment fell on men like German-born Karl Benz and the history of mankind was altered forever. The creation of automobiles fueled the industrial revolution and millions of people around the world became employees of the lucrative automobile business. In America, men like Henry Ford transformed the city of Detroit into the world's largest car manufacturing empire. All the billions of dollars that have been generated by the automotive business is without a doubt part and parcel of the Earth's "fullness." Aha Moment! *The Earth is not suffering from lack but from the absence of men and women of revelation!"*

## QUESTIONS DEMANDING AN ANSWER

If the womb of the Earth is pregnant with God's fullness, why are there so many pockets of lack in the world in which we live? Most importantly, why are there so many of God's children struggling with lack? These are questions that clearly demand an answer. The Holy Spirit told me, *"Much of the lack in this world is due to the unchecked greed of many government and business leaders who are hoarding resources instead of distributing them properly for the common good."* Wealth in the Kingdom of God is based on the concept of "commonwealth." Commonwealth only applies to kingdoms and it implies that in a kingdom all wealth is common to all citizens of the kingdom. Africa, for instance, is one of the richest continents on planet Earth. It is full of mineral, oil and natural resources that could feed the whole continent of Africa for many generations.

There would be no lack or systemic poverty in Africa if these resources were managed properly. Instead, these resources are manipulated and plundered for the benefit of a privileged few. Unfortunately, this scenario is the same in other none-African continents including the developed nations of the so-called first world. Before I migrated to America, I was so naïve as to think that there was no systemic corruption within the institutions of government and business in the United States of America. Boy, was I wrong!

- **Why are there so many pockets of lack in this world?**

   *Speaking to the people, he went on, "Take care! Protect yourself against the least bit of greed. Life is not defined by what you have, even when you have a lot." Then he told them this story: "The farm of a certain rich man produced a terrific crop. He talked to himself: 'What can I do? My barn isn't big enough for this harvest.' Then he said, 'Here's what I'll do: I'll tear down my barns and build bigger ones. Then I'll gather in all my grain and goods, and I'll say to myself, Self, you've done well! You've got it made and can now retire. Take it easy and have the time of your life!'*

*"Just then God showed up and said, 'Fool! Tonight you die. And your barnful of goods—who gets it?' "That's what happens when you fill your barn with Self and not with God." Luke 12:15-21 (MSG)*

The above passage of scripture from the Message Bible helps us answer the question, *why are there so many pockets of the lack in this world?* It is quite clear from the story that Jesus told that the primary culprit behind the many pockets of lack in this world is the green-eyed monster in the hearts of men called "greed." Greed always creates a culture of hoarding in the hearts of men. Instead of distributing the blessings of wealth and prosperity a person has been given by God, people start hoarding everything for themselves.

 **God blessed the Earth with everything needed to sustain life.**

All you need is for a good number of people all over the world to do the same thing (hoarding) and resources that are supposed to be bountiful will suddenly seem scarce. Unfortunately, in most countries, dictatorial presidents pillage their own country of its natural, financial and mineral resources as though these God-ordained natural resources of the country are the private property of one man. As a consequence, there are many pockets of lack and poverty all over the world. The people who are hurt the most by this scenario are the poor, widows and orphans. It's no wonder God is a fiery advocate of the downtrodden in society.

- **Why are there so many of God's children struggling with lack?**

  *My people are destroyed for lack of knowledge. Because you have rejected knowledge, I also will reject you from being priest for Me; Because you have forgotten the law of your God, I also will forget your children. Hosea 4:6*

We are now confronted with having to answer the second question, *Why are there so many of God's children struggling with lack?* It is clear from the testimony of scripture that the Earth is the Lord's and the fullness thereof. In other words, the Earth and the "world" (*the systems of arrangement and order*) belong to the children of the Kingdom. Since this is the case, why are so many of God's children struggling with lack? I believe that the testimony of the Prophet Hosea from the above passage of scripture is the main underlying reason as to why many of God's children are struggling with lack. God makes a decree, "My people are destroyed for lack of knowledge." This means that our lack of knowledge concerning everything that God has already provided for us in His Word is one of the reasons there is so much struggle with lack among God's people.

Once, the Holy Spirit told me that one of the greatest lies the devil has sold us is that "lack" exists on Earth. The Holy Spirit told me that when the scriptures declare, *"the Earth is the Lord's and the fullness thereof,"* it means that the Earth was never created empty. The womb of the Earth is pregnant with God's fullness. The moment we begin to believe the lie that God did not make enough provision for all of us from before the foundation of the world, we open ourselves to a hoarding mentality. This culture of hoarding is birthed by this mindset of scarcity. When a person thinks that resources are limited, the natural tendency is to start hoarding.

## #3. THE WORLD IS THE LORD'S

*The **earth** is the Lord's, and the fullness thereof; the world, and they that dwell therein. (Psalm 24:1)*

The word "world" comes from the Greek word "cosmos" (kosmos). According to Wikipedia, the **cosmos** is the universe regarded as a complex and orderly system; the opposite of chaos. According to

Bishop Tudor Bismark, in his message on the "Power of Weakness," the "world" is the Earth's operating system. We all know that a computer and its operating system are two different things. A computer with a hard-drive without an internal operating system is not much fun. It's like having great potential without much functionality.

According to Biblestudytools.com the word "world" (kosmos) is defined as follows:

1. *An apt and harmonious arrangement or constitution, order, government*
2. *Ornament, decoration, adornment, i.e. the arrangement of the stars, 'the heavenly hosts', as the ornament of the heavens.*

Consequently, when King David, makes the statement, *"the world, and they that dwell therein,"* he is referring to the fact that God owns the operating system behind planet Earth. He also owns *the apt and harmonious arrangement, order, constitution, or government behind our planet.* God also owns the *"ornament, decoration, adornment, i.e. the arrangement of the stars, 'the heavenly hosts', as the ornament of the heavens."* Since it is quite evident that the "world" is a masterful operating system it cannot exist by itself. Like the operating system of any computer, it is embedded inside the Earth's hard-drive. This means that whatever affects the Earth will have a direct impact on the "world," which is the Earth's operating system. This is why when a witch curses your piece of Earth; they can have a drastic effect on your world (*the harmonious arrangement or constitution, order of things in your life*).

 **Why are there so many of God's children struggling with lack?**

On the other hand speaking to the Earth, under the inspiration of the Holy Spirit, can also drastically change your world. Many of you reading this book are going to go through the prayer of activation at the end of this book. You are going to get a chance to *speak faith-filled words* to the Earth beneath your feet and command it to move in your favor. You are going to get an opportunity to dismantle and nullify demonically engineered curses that are working against you from the land beneath your feet. You are going to experience the radical transformation of your world. God's harmonious arrangement, constitution, government and order of things in your life are going to be fully restored. Get ready for a major shift in your life!

## #4. THEY THAT DWELL THEREIN

*The **earth** is the Lord's, and the fullness thereof; the world, and they that dwell therein. (Psalm 24:1)*

The final part of Psalm 24:1 brings us directly into contact with God's ownership of every living person on planet Earth. This passage of scripture flies in the face of the nonsensical theory of evolution in explaining the origins of our species. Darwin's Theory of Evolution states that mankind is an evolved species from a random explosion of matter eons of years ago. Nothing could be further from the truth. Mankind is a product of divine intent and design. The expression ***"The Earth is the Lord's,...and they that dwell therein,"*** implies that every living person on Earth is under God's sovereign jurisdiction and is impacted directly by events that happen to or shape the Earth.

According to Genesis 8:22, the prosperity of the people of this planet is directly connected to the Earth. Genesis 8:22 declares, *while the earth remaineth, seedtime and harvest, and cold and heat, and summer and winter, and day and night shall not cease.* This passage carries the meaning that anything that affects the spiritual or natural conditions of this planet will have a direct impact on man's ability to live a life of prosperity and fulfilled destiny. Have you noticed that each time God chose to bless you financially or materially, He has used someone or something on Earth? I have never seen cars drop out of heaven supernaturally. I have never seen houses drop out of the sky. If you are praying for God to bless you with your "dream house," the Earth is going to have to participate in your miracle or it will never happen.

*For the land is full of adulterers; for because of a curse the land mourns. The pleasant places of the wilderness are dried up. Their course of life is evil, and their might is not right. Jeremiah 23:10*

The above passage of scripture makes it really clear that the land is directly impacted by the sinful behavior of the inhabitants of the Earth. This passage of scripture is very clear that hateful or word curses spoken by people have a direct impact on the Earth's ability to give us the prosperity we need in order to live decent and successful lives. The prophet Jeremiah gives us a very interesting metaphor when he makes the statement, *because of a curse the land mourns.*

Mourning is something we do when we are really sad at the state of things. This means that when the Earth receives a curse from one of the agents of Satan against the saints of the Most High God, the Earth "mourns" the fact that it has to carry out the "curse" against the innocent. However, since Adam (mankind) was given dominion over the Earth, the land has to respond to what men are creating with their words. This means that "Speaking to the Earth" faith-filled words by the children of the Kingdom will go a long way in reversing cycles of curses and iniquity that the Earth is reluctantly trying to process. It goes without saying that whatever has a negative impact on the Earth's divine equilibrium will have an equal and direct impact on man's quality of life. "Speaking to the Earth" is how God's people can continue to influence this precious planet we live on with life-giving words inspired by the Holy Spirit that will cause the Earth to bring forth God's goodness everywhere!

# LIFE APPLICATION SECTION
## MEMORY VERSES

*For the land is full of adulterers; for because of a curse the land mourns. The pleasant places of the wilderness are dried up. Their course of life is evil, and their might is not right. Jeremiah 23:10*

## REFLECTIONS

1. How does the Earth react to curses spoken over it?

_____

_____

_____

_____

_____

_____

2. Why are there so many pockets of lack in the world we live in?

_____

_____

_____

_____

_____

# 3

# Speaking to the Earth

*Give ear, O ye heavens, and I will speak; and hear, O earth, the words of my mouth. Deuteronomy 32:1*

I SINCERELY BELIEVE that one of the most powerful phenomena on Earth is the power of the spoken word. We first observe the power of the spoken word by observing God as He used it to masterfully re-create the Earth. God did not create the Earth by using bulldozers; instead He uses the power of the spoken word. So the first thing that comes out of the mouth of God are the words, "Let there be light!" Immediately after the spoken word, we saw the result of the spoken word as the scriptures plainly declare, "and there was light!" It must not surprise us, therefore, that many of the miracles and the violence that has ever taken place on Earth are directly connected to the spoken word. It is adamantly clear that the spoken word always precedes the creation of something. *This is why the spiritual technology for speaking to the Earth that I am about to share with you in this chapter is very important.*

*Or speak to the earth, and it shall teach thee: and the fishes of the sea shall declare unto thee. Who knoweth not in all*

*these that the hand of the Lord hath wrought this?
(Job 12:8-9)*

*"Francis, what the witches of Africa tried to do to you by speaking
to the Earth in order to place a curse on you is not foreign to Scripture.
It's an ancient spiritual technology for manifesting dominion over the
Earth that God transferred to man in the creation story. Unfortunately,
many of God's children today do not know this powerful ancient
spiritual technology so they rarely ever speak to the Earth.
Consequently, only the children of darkness are constantly speaking
to the Earth, demanding it participates in their evil activities. This is
why the Earth is having convulsions; groaning for the manifestation
of the sons of God who will speak to the Earth to once again line up
with the Kingdom of God and His righteousness" (Romans 8:19-22).*
My regenerated spirit was jumping with excitement as the blessed
Holy Spirit explained this to me. The Holy Spirit showed me that the
Godhead were the first beings to initiate the spiritual technology of
"speaking to the Earth" so as to receive from it whatever they needed
from it. Please observe.

## GOD: THE FIRST EARTH WHISPERER

*And God said, Let the **earth** bring forth grass, the herb
yielding seed, and the fruittree yielding fruit after his kind,
whose seed is in itself, upon the **earth**: and it was so. And
the **earth** brought forth grass, and herb yielding seed after
his kind, and the tree yielding fruit, whose seed was in itself,
after his kind: and God saw that it was good. (Genesis 1:11-
12)*

Please observe that in the above passage of scripture, God was the
first being to speak to the Earth. "Francis, in this Scripture who is God
speaking to? Is He speaking to the angels?" The Holy Spirit asked me
in a gentle but authoritative voice. Why would God speak to the Earth
if it has no ears to hear Him?" The Spirit of God continued to prod my

inquisitive heart. "God was speaking to the Earth!" I declared with all the passion I could muster. "So why don't you and many of my children speak to the Earth to give you whatever you desire that is in accordance with the will of God for your life?" I was stunned and remained speechless. Nevertheless, I was very excited by what the Holy Spirit was saying to me.

 The most powerful phenomena on Earth is the power of the spoken word.

The prophetic implications of what the Holy Spirit was saying to me were limitless and far-reaching. I had never seen the Earth in the same kind of light as I was seeing it under the inspiration of the Holy Spirit. Interestingly enough, speaking to the Earth is a very common practice among members of the New Age. But it dawned on me that Satan is not an originator; he only comes to steal, kill and destroy (John 10:10). Satan is a master at masking what God has already done in order to make it look like the devil's kingdom came up with it. In so doing, the devil has managed to scare away many of God's people from their own inheritance in Christ Jesus simply because a particular activity looks like something the devil and his people would do.

## THE EARTH AND CREATION ARE IN TRAVAIL

*For the earnest expectation of the creation eagerly waits for the revealing of the sons of God. For the creation was subjected to futility, not willingly, but because of Him who subjected it in hope; because the creation itself also will be delivered from the bondage of corruption into the glorious liberty of the children of God. For we know that the whole creation groans and labors with birth pangs together until now. (Romans 8:19-22)*

When it comes to the technology of speaking to the Earth, citizens of the Kingdom of God must place a "demand" on the release of their spiritual inheritance. If God is our Creator and Father, imitating everything He does is not abnormal for us. If we imitate God, we would be simply doing what my friend Sid Roth calls, "being supernaturally normal!" The current situation, in which only the children of wickedness are speaking to the Earth in order to wage war against the saints of the Most High, must not be allowed to continue. Only God knows how many of His dear children experienced untimely deaths because a witch, clairvoyant, sorcerer or wizard spoke a curse of premature death over the soil against them. I know for a fact that if the Holy Spirit had not shown me how to reverse the "hex of premature death" that had been spoken over the soil of Zambia against me, I would have died before my time. I would never have written the book you are holding in your hands.

The above passage of scripture (Romans 8:19-22) clearly shows us that there is a supernatural sense of expectation that God has embedded in all of creation. It was done in such a way that all of creation is eagerly waiting for the manifestation of the sons of God. Since planet Earth is an integral part of the fabric of God's creation; the Earth, like all of creation desperately desires to be delivered from the "bondage of corruption" into the glorious liberty of the children of God. Somehow the Earth seems to know that the key to living up to its highest God given potential is to bring itself under subjection to the rulership of the manifest sons of God.

## POWER SHIFT!

The Holy Spirit continued to flood me with revelation on this powerful spiritual technology. The Holy Spirit showed me that God stopped speaking directly to the Earth (the dust beneath) on the sixth day of creation. "Do you remember what happened on the sixth day of creation?" the Holy Spirit asked me. It did not take me long to figure out what happened on the sixth day of creation. On the sixth day of creation, God created His master specimen – mankind (Adam). He also willingly transferred the legal authority to speak to the Earth to the children of men. Please observe and meditate on the Scriptures below.

> *And God said, Let us make man in our image, after our likeness: and let them have dominion over the fish of the sea, and over the fowl of the air, and over the cattle, and over all the **earth**, and over every creeping thing that creepeth upon the **earth**. (Genesis 1:26)*

The greatest discovery in life is the discovery of purpose. The genesis of God's purpose for creating the human race can be found in the first two chapters of Genesis. The Genesis account underscores God's inherent motivation for creating a physical planet called Earth and creating spirit children that He collectively called "Adam." God then created physical bodies made of dirt (humus) to house these spirit-beings so that they could become legal residents and guardians of the visible world. From the beginning, our physical world (Earth) was designed to be a spiritual colony of the Kingdom of Heaven.

According to Genesis 1:26, God gave Adam five areas of "dominion." We will quickly examine these five areas of dominion:

1. Dominion over the Marine kingdom (over the fish of the sea)
2. Dominion over the Bird kingdom (over the fowl of the air)
3. Dominion over the Animal kingdom (over the cattle)
4. Dominion over the Earth (The Earth's soil, solar system and all its natural resources)
5. Dominion over the Reptilian kingdom (over every creeping thing)

The greatest discovery in life is the discovery of purpose.

Have you noticed that the gifts and callings of God are without repentance? This means that when God transfers spiritual power or gifting, He has no intention of taking them back. Even when we abuse these spiritual gifts and callings, they are still without repentance. This does not mean in any way that we're not going to stand at the judgment Seat of Christ to account for how we used everything God gave us. For people whose names will not be found in the Lamb's book of life, they will still have to account for how they used the power, authority and influence that God gave them during the Great White Throne Judgment (Revelation 21). It suffices to say that if mankind, who was given the dominion over the Earth, does not speak to the Earth to cause it *"to bring forth,"* God will not. The Lord was very clear to me that had I not spoken to the soil of Zambia and reversed the curse that was operating against me, I would have certainly died in Zambia. This is why God hates the spirit of laziness (slothfulness) because God will not do for us what He told us to do for ourselves.

## HOW TO ACTIVATE THIS SPIRITUAL TECHNOLOGY

*And God said, Let the **earth** bring forth grass, the herb yielding seed, and the fruit tree yielding fruit after his kind, whose seed is in itself, upon the **earth**: and it was so. And the **earth** brought forth grass, and herb yielding seed after his kind and the tree yielding fruit, whose seed was in itself, after his kind: and God saw that it was good. (Genesis 1:11-12)*

We will now look at how to activate this spiritual technology of the Kingdom for manifesting dominion on planet Earth. We will use the above passage of scripture as our foundational text. There seems to be five essential elements that come into play when activating this ancient spiritual technology of the Kingdom:

1. **Speaking Faith-filled words...** This is crystalized in the statement "And God said!" This means that the initiator of this spiritual technology initiates it by speaking in faith.

2. **Speaking directly to the Earth to cause it to bring forth...** This is crystalized in the statement "let the Earth bring forth!" This means that the initiator of this spiritual technology needs to live in hopeful anticipation of the Earth bringing forth what has been requested in Jesus name.

3. **Declaring without wishful ambiguity...** This is crystalized in the statement *"bring forth grass, the herb yielding seed, and the fruit tree yielding fruit after his kind, whose seed is in itself, upon the **Earth**: and it was so."* The initiator of this spiritual technology must declare without any ambiguity exactly what he or she requires the Earth to bring forth.

4. **Believing that the Earth has heard...**your faith decrees in the presence of God. This is crystallized in the statement, *"and it was so."*

5. **Waiting in holy anticipation...** for the Earth to bring forth what was requested of it, in the spirit of faith. This is crystallized in the statement *"And the **Earth** brought forth grass, and herb yielding seed after his kind, and the tree yielding fruit, whose seed was in itself, after his kind."*

The last chapter of this book is all about prophetic activation of readers of this book, in the prophetic act of speaking to the Earth. By the grace of God I have designed a very powerful, Holy Spirit inspired prayer of activation that I want to take you through. This prayer of activation incorporates all of the five aspects of this powerful spiritual technology of the Kingdom of God. The final part of this book deals with testimonials. There have been many miracles that have taken place in the lives of so many of God's people around the world because of this revelation of speaking to the Earth. You will also learn about how God used the prophetic act of speaking to the Earth to topple a ruthless dictator over an entire country. You will be blessed and refreshed by these miraculous testimonies from around the world. I really believe that the Earth beneath your feet is about to shift in your favor. All unnecessary struggles and demonic attacks that you have been going through will be brought to an abrupt end. Get ready to rejoice in the Lord!

## Taking Authority!!!

*The heaven, even the heavens, are the Lord's: but the earth hath he given to the children of men. (Psalms 115:16)*

According to the above passages of scripture, God transferred "the authority and rights of usage" to this ancient and powerful spiritual technology of speaking to the Earth to Adam, the first Kingdom ambassador. Consequently, the "children of men" are now the proud owners of one of the most powerful spiritual technologies on Earth: **"Speaking to the Earth to cause it to bring forth!"** *"Francis, when you speak to the Earth to bring forth or swallow something, you must have faith in God and be very specific in what you desire it to bring forth. Just remember that God's kingdom will not support unrighteousness or anything that does not line up with God's will for your life. When We spoke to the Earth to bring forth, We were very specific in what We wanted it to bring forth!"* The Holy Spirit declared emphatically.

## Out of the Dust Back to the Dust!

*In the sweat of thy face shalt thou eat bread, till thou return unto the ground; for out of it wast thou taken: for dust thou art, and unto dust shalt thou return. (Genesis 3:19)*

I have learned over the years of walking with God that if I don't fully understand something the "Holy Spirit" is doing, He will graciously guide me into all truth. I asked the Holy Spirit to tell me why the spell of the witches of Africa spoken over the dust of the ground could affect my physical body in such a dreadful way? The Holy Spirit's response was swift and amazingly scriptural. By the time the Holy Spirit finished explaining, I was simply dazzled, inspired and reminded of the Scripture in Hosea that says, *"My people are destroyed for the lack of knowledge"* (Hosea 4:6). I will try to rephrase what the Holy Spirit once told me.

The Holy Spirit said to me, *"Francis, you were created with a body of dust that houses your spirit. Since you have a body of dust that originates from the Earth, any demonically empowered witchcraft spells spoken over the dust of the ground against you can have a drastic impact on your well-being unless you (as the redeemed of the Lord) give the Earth (the dust beneath) a higher and righteous instruction than the one its been given to obey by the children of wickedness."* I was stunned by Holy Spirit's revelation. I had never heard this before. I was hungry for more revelation on this subject. I was not disappointed because there were more scriptures from the Holy Spirit to explain what I had experienced in Zambia on that fateful night. In the coming chapters, I will dive into many of those scriptures.

# LIFE APPLICATION SECTION
# MEMORY VERSES

*In the sweat of thy face shalt thou eat bread, till thou return unto the ground; for out of it wast thou taken: for dust thou art, and unto dust shalt thou return. (Genesis 3:19)*

# REFLECTIONS

1. Write down five things to consider before speaking to the Earth?

_____

_____

_____

_____

_____

_____

2. Why can a witchcraft spell spoken over the soil against a child of God, do them harm?

_____

_____

_____

_____

_____

_____

# 4

# Man's Dominion Over the Earth

*The heaven, even the heavens, are the Lord's: but the earth
hath he given to the children of men. Psalms 115:16*

THE GREATEST DISCOVERY in life is the discovery of
purpose. The genesis of God's purpose for creating the
human race can be found in the first two chapters of Genesis.
The Genesis account underscores God's inherent motivation for
creating a physical planet called Earth and creating spirit children that
He collectively called "Adam." God then created physical bodies
made of dirt (humus) to house these spirit-beings so that they could
become legal residents and guardians of the visible world. From the
beginning, our physical world (Earth) was designed to be a spiritual
colony of the Kingdom of Heaven ruled by the manifest sons of God.

*Then God said, "Let Us make man in Our image, according
to Our likeness; let them have dominion over the fish of the*

*sea, over the birds of the air, and over the cattle, over all the earth and over every creeping thing that creeps on the earth." So God created man in His own image; in the image of God He created him; male and female He created them. Then God blessed them, and God said to them, "Be fruitful and multiply; fill the earth and subdue it; have dominion over the fish of the sea, over the birds of the air, and over every living thing that moves on the earth" (Genesis 1:26-28 NKJV).*

"Francis, had you not spoken to the Earth when I told you to, you would have died in Zambia." I was stunned. But I asked the Holy Spirit why? As He always does with me, the Holy Spirit took me back to the Word of God. The Bible says that God has placed His Word above His name (Psalm 138:2). This means that since the name of God represents His nature and character, it suffices to say that God highly esteems His Word. This means that once God establishes a biblical principle and precedence, He never violates it.

The Holy Spirit asked me another equally important question to help me understand the statement He made to me. "Francis, when did God stop speaking to the Earth in the book of Genesis?" Before I could answer, the Holy Spirit declared, "On the sixth day of creation!" I went to the book of Genesis and read the entire first chapter and then I saw it! From Genesis 1:11-25, God was speaking to the Earth to bring forth whatever He desired. However, on the sixth day of creation, God created His best specimen yet. God created Adam (man) in His exact image and likeness and transferred legal authority over the planet to him. Adam immediately became the new incoming administration over planet Earth.

## GIFTS & CALLINGS

*For the gifts and the calling of God are irrevocable. (Romans 11:29)*

What is interesting to note on the day that God created mankind is the gifts and calling God gave him. Without any undue pressure from anybody, God decided to gift mankind with the gift of dominion over the Earth and all her resources. This gift of dominion that God gave to Mankind gave us the power to affect the Earth in four distinct ways:

1. *Be fruitful and*
2. *Multiply;*
3. *Fill the Earth and*
4. *Subdue it;*

Firstly, *man has the power to command the Earth to be fruitful.* This aspect of man's dominion over this planet is the reason why there should be no lack on Earth. Man has the power within the sound of his voice, especially when he is divinely inspired by God, to *cause the Earth to bring forth.* Empowered by the Holy Spirit, mankind can cause *the Earth to bring forth fruit.* What is of note is that *fruit* is an end product. Fruit is always the by-product of the planted seed. This begs the question, "Where is the seed that is causing the Earth to be fruitful?" The answer is strikingly powerful. How did God cause the Earth to be fruitful in the first place? According to the Genesis account, God spoke the Word and the spoken Word became the "spermatic seed" that impregnated the Earth to *bring forth everything God desired.*

Once God establishes a biblical principle and precedence, He never violates it.

This is the exact same gift that God gave or transferred to Adam. According to Romans 11:29, once God gave this special calling and gift to mankind; He could never revoke it. Man would forever have the power to command the Earth to be fruitful and bring forth. Once this gift of dominion was transferred to man, the Earth has no choice but to heed the voice of a man. This means that the Earth has to process the seeds of the spoken words of men in order to bring them forth. This is why when a person's "confession" is continually calling out for death, it should not surprise us that the Earth responds by bringing forth death in their life by any means necessary. The light bulb of revelation went off in my head and I realized that I had to speak to the Earth in Zambia for my own deliverance. The reason was simple; through the spoken word, I was carrying the "seed" that the Earth needed to bring forth my own deliverance from premature death. This is precisely why this book you're reading is extremely important to re-establishing your dominion of planet Earth. Remember: You are a walking "warehouse of seed" that the Earth requires in order to bring forth everything God attached to your destiny. It is time for you to speak to the Earth and see her shift in your favor!

## MULTIPLY

Secondly, *man has the power and legal authority to multiply himself and what he wants on Earth.* This aspect of man's dominion over this planet is the reason God only created two individuals, male and female. *He created them male and female, and blessed them and called them Mankind in the day they were created (Genesis 5:2).* Is it not simply amazing that the over five billion people on our planet came out of two humans? I am so glad that God did not create them Adam and Steve or there would have been no procreation (multiplication). Procreation is the visible example of mankind multiplying himself.

On the other hand, mankind also has the power to multiply on Earth whatsoever he needs. For instance, Henry Ford came up with one car but when he realized that there was a way to duplicate the process so as to get the car in the hands of millions of customers, he went into a holy frenzy manufacturing cars, transforming the city of Detroit into Motor City. What we must not forget is that everything that goes into the making of a car comes from the Earth beneath our feet. So, in essence, when a cellphone company mass produces these devices from materials obtained from the Earth beneath, they are in essence answering God's call in the book of Genesis for man to multiply and replenish the Earth.

Unfortunately, man's God-given power to multiply can also be used against him by the devil. Ever since the fall of man, mankind has also been "multiplying" things that are destroying the moral and structural integrity of the Earth. For instance, one of the reasons God destroyed the old world through a massive flood (besides the sin of fallen angels sleeping with women) was because the Earth was filled with violence. *The earth also was corrupt before God, and the earth was filled with violence (Genesis 6:11).* This verse explains why terrorism is running rampart across the Middle East and other nations; the more you have the soldiers of Jihad in the Muslim world promising more acts of terror against infidels, terrorism naturally multiplies. This is a deranged misuse of God's gift to man to "multiply!"

## REPLENISH THE EARTH

Thirdly, mankind carries a God-given capacity to *"fill or replenish the Earth!"* The word "replenish" carries the following meaning:

1. *To make full or complete again, as by supplying what is lacking, used up, etc.:*
2. *To supply (a fire, stove, etc.) with fresh fuel.*
3. *To fill again or anew.*

Since man's dominion mandate carries the ability to "replenish or fill the Earth," it becomes increasingly important for us to realize the power "the spoken word" has over the Earth. We can choose to "fill again" the Earth's atmosphere with "hate or racism" and reap bloodshed. On the other hand, we can choose to replenish the Earth with "Love, faith, and hope!" If we do so, we are going to have a planet we will all enjoy living on. This is why the technology of speaking to the Earth under the inspiration of the Holy Spirit is so critical in this season.

 **What we must not forget is that everything that goes into the making of a car comes from the Earth.**

Fourthly, mankind carries the supernatural grace and gifting to "subdue the Earth." Let us first define the word, "subdue." According to dictionary.com the word "subdue" carries the following meaning:

1. *To conquer and bring into subjection:*
2. *To overpower by superior force; overcome.*
3. *To bring under mental or emotional control, as by persuasion or intimidation; render submissive.*
4. *To repress (feelings, impulses, etc.).*
5. *To bring (land) under cultivation: (to subdue the wilderness.)*
6. *To reduce the intensity, force, or vividness of (sound, light, color, etc.); tone down; soften.*

It is quite clear that God gave man the supernatural ability *to subdue the Earth.* The above definitions of the word "subdue" gives us a working model concerning the scope, height and breadth of man's dominion mandate. We now know from studying this word that to *subdue something* means that you have *the power to bring that thing under subjection.* Perhaps it is this aspect of man's dominion over the Earth that is the underlying reason why the Lord allowed me to go through what I went through in Zambia: so that I can be reminded to take my responsibility of subduing the Earth seriously.

When the witches in Zambia spoke to the dirt (Earth) and *released a curse of premature death against me*, they were, in essence, subduing the Earth. In their case, they were subduing the Earth to line up with the power and kingdom of darkness. The reason the Holy Spirit told me to also speak to the Earth was so that I could subdue the Earth with a new instruction that is connected to a higher order of government, the government of the Kingdom of God. In other words, when I spoke to the Earth (soil) in Zambia, I released it from being subdued by a witchcraft spell. Perhaps this is the reason why the Earth and all of creation are travailing for the manifestation of the sons of God so that *all of creation can be delivered from the bondage of corruption into the glorious liberty of the children of God* (Romans 8:19). I sincerely believe that the Earth is crying (groaning) for the "manifest sons of God" to subdue it in righteousness. After all the Earth was created by God and for God's purpose. Why would it want to swallow "iniquity" everyday? The Earth is travailing to enter the realm of "Shalom!"

# LIFE APPLICATION SECTION
## MEMORY VERSES

*Then God said, "Let Us make man in Our image, according to Our likeness; let them have dominion over the fish of the sea, over the birds of the air, and over the cattle, over all the earth and over every creeping thing that creeps on the earth." So God created man in His own image; in the image of God He created him; male and female He created them. Then God blessed them, and God said to them, "Be fruitful and multiply; fill the earth and subdue it; have dominion over the fish of the sea, over the birds of the air, and over every living thing that moves on the earth." (Genesis 1:26-28 NKJV)*

# REFLECTIONS

1. What does the word "subdue" mean in Man's dominion mandate?

_____

_____

_____

_____

_____

2. What does the word "replenish" mean in Man's dominion mandate?

_____

_____

_____

_____

# 5

# Earth: The First Witness

*I call heaven and earth to record this day against you, that*
*I have set before you life and death, blessing and cursing:*
*therefore choose life, that both thou and thy seed may live.*
*Deuteronomy 30:19*

WHEN THE LORD was giving me the revelation of "speaking to the Earth," He showed me something that I had not seen before. He showed me a governing principle that I state below. The Lord showed me that the Earth (Ground) is the first witness in the dishing out of divine blessings or judgment. When the Lord showed me this governing principle, I started to see it play out throughout the bible. I will give you several examples of this governing principle in other passages of scripture.

### *Principle # The Earth/Ground is the first witness*
### *in the dishing out of divine blessings or judgment:*

# THE FIRST WITNESS

We have all heard of the word, "witness." The word "witness" is a very powerful word in the legal community. In a court of law, a witness can sentence a person to a lifetime of imprisonment or cause an accused person to be set free. It all depends on the credibility of the witness and the information they have for or against the accused. To help us appreciate this fact, let us define the word, "witness." According to dictionary.com, these are some of the definitions I found interesting and applicable to our study:

1. *To bear witness to;*

2. *Testify to;*

3. *Give or afford evidence of.*

4. *A person or thing that affords evidence.*

If we conjoin the above definitions of the word "witness" as it relates to man's relationship with the Earth, we end up with a very interesting body of thought. Since the Earth is the first witness to nature's reaction to man's obedience or disobedience to God's authority, we can't take the Earth's reaction lightly. When Adam and Eve committed high treason against the government of God, the first violent reaction against them came from the Earth beneath their feet. The ground (soil) beneath their feet came under a curse for their sake. A "curse," a foreign and demonic entity, attached itself to man's ability to cultivate the Earth. Instead of giving man the plushy green lawns, which characterized the Garden of Eden, the land began to give birth to thorns and thistles. In a prophetic sense, the condition of the Earth is a divine indicator of whether we are under divine approval or disapproval.

*And unto Adam he said, Because thou hast hearkened unto the voice of thy wife, and hast eaten of the tree, of which I commanded thee, saying, Thou shalt not eat of it: cursed is the ground for thy sake; in sorrow shalt thou eat of it all the days of thy life; Thorns also and thistles shall it bring forth to thee; and thou shalt eat the herb of the field; In the sweat of thy face shalt thou eat bread, till thou return unto the ground; for out of it wast thou taken: for dust thou art, and unto dust shalt thou return. (Genesis 3:17-19)*

## WHAT IN GOD'S NAME IS GOING ON?

*Now there was a famine in the days of David for three years, year after year; and David inquired of the Lord. And the Lord answered, "It is because of Saul and his bloodthirsty house, because he killed the Gibeonites." So the king called the Gibeonites and spoke to them. Now the Gibeonites were not of the children of Israel, but of the remnant of the Amorites; the children of Israel had sworn protection to them, but Saul had sought to kill them in his zeal for the children of Israel and Judah. Therefore David said to the Gibeonites, "What shall I do for you? And with what shall I make atonement, that you may bless the inheritance of the Lord?" (2 Samuel 21:1-3)*

Any self-respecting biblical scholar will tell you that the first testimony of God about David is that he was a man after the heart of God. Even before the Bible gave us the name of this amazing character, we are first told that he was a man after the heart of God. It didn't take long for us to quickly discover why God called David a man after the heart of God. Without a doubt, David was a passionate lover of God. King David wrote many of the romantic songs and Psalms in the Bible. David had such a close walk with God; he was referred to as a friend of God. God would constantly compare the kings of Israel who came after David to David. In other words, King David became the gold standard for "kingship" in ancient Israel. This is what makes the above passage of Scripture a very interesting study

The Earth is the first witness in the dishing out of divine blessings or judgment.

When King David took the reins of power in Israel, many of his subjects were very happy indeed. The coronation of King David over the twelve tribes of Israel was the beginning of a new era. David quickly restored the lost Ark of the Covenant from the land of the Philistines. He quickly pitched a simple tent in the city of David for the Ark of the Covenant, thereby establishing a new order of worship in Israel. This simple tent would later be referred to as the Tabernacle of David. However, the immediate reaction of the Earth to David's godly reign did not make any sense at all. Even though no one could dispute the fact that David was a godly king, there was a severe famine in the land of Israel for three consecutive years. Thankfully, unlike many of today's political leaders, King David knew instinctively that the famine in the land might be an indicator of divine disapproval of some kind.

King David went before the Lord and inquired of the Lord. He wanted to know the reason behind the severe famine. The Lord, in His eternal goodness, did not disappoint. He quickly told King David that the reason the land was not yielding its usual bountifulness was because of the sin of King Saul. David's predecessor had committed a great injustice against the Gibeonites. The Gibeonites were a nation of slaves in Israel who had deceived Joshua many generations earlier into entering into a covenant with Israel in the name of Yahweh. Joshua was very upset with the Gibeonites when he discovered their deception and yet he couldn't violate the covenant he had just made with them in the name of the God of Israel. Instead, he made them into a nation of slaves but an Israeli sword could never be used to kill any of them, without just cause.

# Breaking Generational Land Curses

*But when the inhabitants of Gibeon heard what Joshua had done to Jericho and Ai, they worked craftily, and went and pretended to be ambassadors. And they took old sacks on their donkeys, old wineskins torn and mended, old and patched sandals on their feet, and old garments on themselves; and all the bread of their provision was dry and moldy. And they went to Joshua, to the camp at Gilgal, and said to him and to the men of Israel, "We have come from a far country; now therefore, make a covenant with us." Then the men of Israel said to the Hivites, "Perhaps you dwell among us; so how can we make a covenant with you?" But they said to Joshua, "We are your servants." And Joshua said to them, "Who are you, and where do you come from?" Joshua 9:3-7*


*So they said to him: "From a very far country your servants have come, because of the name of the Lord your God; for we have heard of His fame, and all that He did in Egypt, and all that He did to the two kings of the Amorites who were beyond the Jordan—to Sihon king of Heshbon, and Og king of Bashan, who was at Ashtaroth. Therefore our elders and all the inhabitants of our country spoke to us, saying, 'Take provisions with you for the journey, and go to meet them, and say to them, "We are your servants; now therefore, make a covenant with us.'" This bread of ours we took hot for our provision from our houses on the day we departed to come to you. But now look, it is dry and moldy. And these wineskins which we filled were new, and see, they are torn; and these our garments and our sandals have become old because of the very long journey." Then the men of Israel took some of their provisions; but they did not ask counsel of the Lord. So Joshua made peace with them, and made a covenant with them to let them live; and the rulers of the congregation swore to them. (Joshua 9:8-15)*

The covenant between the children of Israel and the Gibeonites went unbroken for many generations until the unfortunate reign of King Saul. King Saul had no understanding, nor respect for spiritual protocol. He went ahead and executed many Gibeonites because it made him look good politically. Unfortunately, his actions opened a spiritual portal for demons of famine to enter the Promise Land. Once a seed is "sown" it starts to germinate in "time" until the time of maturation. It almost seemed like the people and land of Israel were not going to be affected by the covenant-breaking spirit of King Saul. Unfortunately this was not the case.

After the death of King Saul and the coronation of David as king, there rose a very severe famine that struck the land of Israel. This famine went unabated for three solid years and would have continued had King David not sought the Lord's face. The famine brought tremendous stress and hardships in the life of the people of Israel. Additionally the famine almost destroyed the national economy. David cried to the Lord and sought a divine solution to the national crisis. God's answer was swift and to the point. And the Lord answered, *"It is because of Saul and his bloodthirsty house because he killed the Gibeonites."*

King David knew instinctively that the famine in the land might be an indicator of divine disapproval of some kind.

## THE POWER OF A PRINCIPLE

What is quite interesting about the scriptural passage 2 Samuel 21:1-3 is the governing principle it establishes. *It establishes the principle that the sinful actions of political leaders can unleash curses or divine judgment on the land that can affect the life of the citizenry drastically.* I will go into greater details about this irrefutable principle in the chapter titled, *Redeeming the Land.* We have already established the fact that each time mankind violates God's authority; the Earth is the first witness to God's displeasure. So when *the land of milk and honey* (Israel) stopped producing fruit for three consecutive years, King David was wise enough to know that the problem was based on a broken spiritual principle. It is wisdom to know when its time to enter into a period of repentance.

David inquired of the Lord so he could get an accurate divine prognosis of the ills of the nation. After the Lord told him that it was the national sin of executing the Gibeonites that was at the heart of the famine, King David wasted no time getting an audience with the leaders of the Gibeonites. David asked for their forgiveness on behalf of the struggling nation and asked them to name the price of restitution. This is what the Scripture says about the two questions David asked the Gibeonites. *"What shall I do for you? And with what shall I make atonement, that you may bless the inheritance of the Lord?"* The Gibeonites did not hesitate in naming the price of restitution.

## THE PRICE OF RESTITUTION

*And the Gibeonites said to him, "We will have no silver or gold from Saul or from his house, nor shall you kill any man in Israel for us." So he said, "Whatever you say, I will do for you." Then they answered the king, "As for the man who consumed us and plotted against us, that we should be destroyed from remaining in any of the territories of Israel, let seven men of his descendants be delivered to us, and we will hang them before the Lord in Gibeah of Saul, whom the Lord chose." And the king said, "I will give them" (2 Samuel 21:4-6).* The Gibeonites asked King David to give them permission to kill seven men of the descendants of King Saul. They did not want the sword of death to fall on innocent Israelites who were just following the orders of a deranged king. Except for Mephibosheth (Jonathan's disabled-son), King David handed the remaining male descendants of King Saul's family to the Gibeonites.

The Gibeonites wasted no time in dishing out their version of justice. They hanged the male descendants of King Saul on a hill for everyone to see. What is most interesting is the statement that follows this event in the final part of the fourteenth verse of 2 Samuel 21. It reads, *"and after that, God heeded the prayer for the land."* This statement carries the meaning that God was not going to remove the curse of famine on the land until after this very important restitution. There is much to learn for all of us here. Nevertheless, I am so glad that we are under the covenant of grace and not law where restitution was based on the premise of, *"an eye for an eye and tooth for tooth!"*

## REPENTANCE BEFORE SPEAKING TO THE EARTH

*If we say that we have no sin, we deceive ourselves, and the truth is not in us. If we confess our sins, He is faithful and just to forgive us our sins and to cleanse us from all unrighteousness. (1 John 1:8-9)*

Repentance is one of the most powerful spiritual technologies for effecting spiritual recovery. This is why the message of John the Baptist was very simple. *"Repent for the Kingdom of Heaven is at hand"* was his daily mantra to those who came to hear him speak. He knew, as an officer of the Kingdom of God, that *repentance* w as heaven's reset button. The writer of the book of 1 John also agrees. 1 John 1:8-9 is one of my favorite passages in the Bible. John, the beloved, makes a very powerful statement: *If we say that we have no sin, we deceive ourselves and the truth is not in us.* I know this statement is very difficult to swallow by those who are encumbered by religious pride. Please remember, John the apostle was writing to born-again believers when he wrote the book of first John. This was not an epistle that was addressed to heathens (non-believers).

My favorite part is the last part of the passage (verse 9), which says, *"If we confess our sins, He is faithful and just to forgive us our sins and to cleanse us from all unrighteousness."* I just think that this is one of the most gracious scriptures in the Bible. This Scripture shows us the true heart of God. God is not a God who is hiding in the bushes waiting to pounce on us should we fall into the quicksand of sin. I believe that it would be wise to do some prayerful reflection before attempting to *speak to the Earth to release prosperity.* Maybe the troubles or famine in our lives could be the direct result of having sinned against God or violated other innocent people. Should the blessed Holy Spirit show us that such is the case, *we need to repent and ask God for forgiveness.* We have to run under the covering of the shed blood of Christ so that our sins can be wiped away. How can the Earth beneath our feet respond to our God-given authority over it; if we are living in disobedience towards God? I do not believe disobedience to God is a winning strategy for any child of God. In some cases, the Lord may even lead us to do some form of physical restitution in order for Him to ***heal and give us the good of the land (Isaiah 1:19).***

# LIFE APPLICATION SECTION
## MEMORY VERSES

*Israel took some of their provisions; but they did not ask counsel of the Lord. So Joshua made peace with them, and made a covenant with them to let them live; and the rulers of the congregation swore to them. (Joshua 9:3-15)*

# REFLECTIONS

1. Why was there three consecutive years of famine during King David's reign?

_____

_____

_____

_____

_____

_____

2. What is restitution?

_____

_____

_____

_____

_____

_____

# 6

# The Earth's Face
# and Mouth

*And the Lord said unto Cain, Where is Abel thy brother?
And he said I know not: Am I my brother's keeper? And he
said, what hast thou done? The voice of thy brother's blood
crieth unto me from the ground. (Genesis 4:9-10)*

THIS REVELATION ON speaking to the Earth and the
nature of the Earth itself deepens once we get to the fourth
chapter of the book of Genesis. What we will discover about
the spiritual nature of "Earth" will almost sound far-fetched
and borderline "new age" if it was not for the fact that the
information we will be examining is found in the Holy Bible. What is
quite interesting to me is that it is God and Adam's rebellious son,
Cain, who will introduce us to *the two facets of the Earth* that we
will be examining in this chapter.

The fourth chapter of Genesis opens with God confronting Cain
about the whereabouts of his younger brother, Abel. Cain's
answer was prideful, daring and contemptuous to say the least. The
fact that he lived through the encounter with God and was not struck

down like the arrogant King Herod (Acts 12) is a sure testament to God's amazing grace. King Herod died instantly and began to rot when an angel of God killed him for taking the glory of God for himself. Cain was truly a prideful person. Who talks to the living God with that kind of in-your-face disrespect and lives to tell the story? It's no wonder Cain is referred to as being of the evil one by the apostle John (1 John 3:12).

## THE BLOOD CRIES OUT!

*And he said, what hast thou done? The voice of thy brother's blood crieth unto me from the ground. (Genesis 4:10)*

God asked Cain a question worth repeating here. "What have you done?" This question tells us a lot about God and gives us a glimpse into a prerequisite redeeming principle for "Healing the Land." We will examine this redemptive principle fully in the chapter titled, *Redeeming the Land*. However, it suffices to say that the question God asked Cain implies implicitly that God never initiates the healing process until man takes responsibility for what he or she has done. This same question, *"What have you done?"* was first given to Adam and Eve when they fell from their exalted position of dominion in the Garden of Eden. *"And the Lord God said to the woman, "What is this you have done?" (Genesis 3:13)*

Before Cain could answer, the Lord made another very important statement that gives us another equally important "redeeming" principle. *"The voice of thy brother's blood crieth unto me from the ground,"* the Lord declared. It's the first time in Scripture we are told that blood "carries" a distinctive sound frequency in the spirit-world unique to the individual whose blood it is. This statement is truly amazing because it was before the advent of forensic science and the discovery of DNA. Here is the redeeming principle: *"Whenever innocent blood is shed on Earth and mixes with the ground, both the blood and the land enjoin into a deafening cry for justice before the Courts of heaven!"* Once again, we will discuss this redemptive principle in greater detail in the chapter on, *Redeeming the Land*.

# CURSED FROM THE EARTH!

*And now art thou cursed from the earth, which hath opened her mouth to receive thy brother's blood from thy hand; (Genesis 4:11)*

This divine interaction between Cain and the Almighty God is loaded with redeeming or prerequisite principles for redeeming the land and breaking lingering curses on the land. In this particular instance, God establishes an immutable and universal "punitive principle" when He boldly declares, *"And now art thou cursed from the Earth, which hath opened her mouth to receive thy brother's blood from thy hand."* God establishes a punitive principle for which there is no door of escape outside of heartfelt repentance and applying the shed blood of Jesus, which is the only blood in our universe that transcends and satisfies the cry for justice of any other shed blood *(to Jesus the mediator of the new covenant, and to the blood of sprinkling that speaks better things than that of Abel, Hebrews 12:24).* In most law-abiding nations, the punitive principle that God attached to the shedding of innocent blood usually results in either a "death or life-long prison sentence." *This ancient punitive principle is an integral part of the penal code of all law-abiding nations.* Some liberal thinkers find the death penalty despicable but God knows best. If the one who created "life" says a life for a life, He knows what He is talking about.

*When thou tillest the ground, it shall not henceforth yield unto thee her strength; a fugitive and a vagabond shalt thou be in the Earth. (Genesis 4:12)*

What got my attention when I was studying through this passage of Scripture in light of what happened to me in Zambia was the phrase *"And now art thou cursed from the Earth!"* The Holy Spirit immediately had me take note of this important fact: the "curse" that came upon Cain for what he did; did not come from God or heaven above. Cain's vagabond curse came from the Earth (soil) beneath his feet. The Lord showed me that a "curse" could either be on the land itself or come directly from the Earth (land) against someone, a family or a people group. Having grown up in Africa, I know for a fact that stories were told where a witch took some dirt in her hands, cursed it and threw it against the building of a thriving business or farm and the business suddenly went into bankruptcy or great misfortunes befell its owners. I had just never seen this in the Bible! We will fully examine, how a curse on the land or from the land operates in the next chapter, *Redeeming the Land.*

Whenever innocent blood is shed on Earth and mixes with the ground, a curse is released!

## HER MOUTH! WHAT IS THIS?

*And now art thou cursed from the earth, which hath opened her mouth to receive thy brother's blood from thy hand; (Genesis 4:11)*

While there is so much to chew on here, what left me speechless was what God told Cain. God tells him succinctly, "You are NOW (at that exact moment) cursed from the Earth, which has OPENED HER MOUTH!!!" Did you catch that statement? This expression by God sounds weird and borderline "new age." I couldn't believe what I was seeing as the Holy Spirit soaked my spirit in divine revelation. "What do you mean God? Are you telling me that the Earth beneath my feet has a mouth?" I asked incredulously.

"Yes, it has!" came the Holy Spirit's reply. "Francis, the Earth not only has a mouth but it's also a "she" because like any woman with a womb, she (Earth) can bring forth the SEED to full term (HARVEST)!" I was speechless. The Word of God was beginning to taste like honey in my mouth. It dawned on me that God was using a "feminine pronoun" (her) to describe the Earth. We will discuss the Earth's feminine nature in great detail in the next chapter. It suffices to say that I was getting more from God on this amazing subject than I had expected. I can only say at this juncture that it's the Earth's feminine nature that makes "speaking to the Earth" even plausible.

## THE FACE OF THE EARTH! WHAT IS THIS?

*And Cain said unto the Lord, My punishment is greater than I can bear. Behold, thou hast driven me out this day from the face of the earth; and from thy face shall I be hid; and I shall be a fugitive and a vagabond in the earth; and it shall come to pass, that every one that findeth me shall slay me. (Genesis 4:13-14)*

When Cain finally responded to the divine inquisition, what he says to God after hearing his sentence baffled me even further. *"Behold, thou hast driven me out this day from the face of the Earth;"* was Cain's petrified response. Cain makes a startling statement that the Earth has a face, just as God has a face. The fact that God never bothered to challenge Cain's assertions means that his statement was true. Now, one could say this expression "face" may be referring to the surface of the Earth but in this case, it would not be plausible because even though Cain was banished from the presence of God, he still had contact with the Earth's surface.

Nevertheless, I am also not suggesting in any way that the Earth has "personality" like humans do, because it does not have that kind of attribute. Notwithstanding, it would seem that God, the creator of the universe, treats the Earth as an "entity" or an "it" that is both alive and has presence (*presence: in the case of the Earth is a simple reference to its divinely embedded ability to react to man's obedience or disobedience to God, as though it sees man's actions*). Since God is the only and ultimate Source of life, we have to assume then that anything that is capable of bringing forth life is somehow intricately connected at some level to the only life giver, -God.

 I was speechless, and the Word of God was begin ning to taste like honey in my mouth.

The expression *"you have driven me from the "face of the Earth"* also makes sense if the expression was Cain's way of saying that God had enshrined him to a life on Earth where he would never experience the "force of favor" from the Earth directed towards him. Whichever way you slice this apple, the "Earth" is much more than we are led to believe in our study of the Earth's topography. Since the Lord Jesus already told us we live in a Kingdom driven by mystery (*He replied, "The knowledge of the mysteries of the kingdom of heaven has been given to you, but not to them. Matthew 13:11*), my money is on the expression, ***"there is more to this planet than meets the eye!"*** Have you ever wondered why all outer space explorations conducted by astronauts have yet to find another planet in our solar system that can sustain life like the planet Earth?

# LIFE APPLICATION SECTION
## MEMORY VERSES

*And the Lord said unto Cain, Where is Abel thy brother? And he said I know not: Am I my brother's keeper? And he said, what hast thou done? The voice of thy brother's blood crieth unto me from the ground. (Genesis 4:9-10)*

# REFLECTIONS

1. What caused Cain to kill Abel his brother?

_____

_____

_____

_____

_____

_____

2. What did the ground do to Cain for spilling innocent blood?

_____

_____

_____

_____

_____

# 7

# Mother Earth: Vomiting & Swallowing

*And now art thou cursed from the earth, which hath opened* ***her*** *mouth to receive thy brother's blood from thy hand; (Genesis 4:11)*

IN THE PREVIOUS chapter, I started to address the fact that God Almighty treats the Earth as though "she is a she." Let me once again restate here what the Spirit of God told me when He started to entrust me with this "Earth moving" revelation. "Francis, the Earth not only has a mouth, but it's also a "she" because like any woman with a womb, she can bring forth the SEED to full term (HARVEST)!" I want you to pause and meditate on the previous statement. It's quite obvious, the God who created the Earth before He created mankind does not treat it or see it the same way we do. The question that quickly comes to my mind is simply this, "Who knows the Earth best? God or man?" It's an easy choice for me, - God!

The Late Dr. Myles Munroe used to say, "Purpose is always hidden in the mind of the manufacturer of a product." Planet Earth is without question, God's creation. In the beginning, God created the heavens and the earth, Genesis 1:1. So when the creator or manufacturer of a product addresses a product we thought we knew differently from how we have always perceived it, the burden of realigning our thinking is on us and not on God, since God is the Creator (manufacturer) in this case. So when the Holy Spirit showed me that God calls the Earth a "her," I knew instantly that if I wanted to be truly successful on Earth, it was incumbent upon me to know why God uses the feminine pronoun to address something that I had treated as an inanimate object.

## THE WOMB OF THE EARTH

*Then God said, "Let the earth bring forth grass, the herb that yields seed, and the fruit tree that yields fruit according to its kind, whose seed is in itself, on the earth"; and it was so. And the earth brought forth grass, the herb that yields seed according to its kind, and the tree that yields fruit, whose seed is in itself according to its kind. And God saw that it was good. (Genesis 1:11-12)*

The above passage of Scripture makes it overwhelmingly clear that in the beginning, God created the Earth with the ability for "womb." This begs the very important question, "What is a womb?" A womb is anything that is capable of conceiving **seed** and then nurturing that **seed** until its time of **maturation** and **highest potential** of existence is actualized. Anything that can do that has a WOMB.

Prophetically, but not theologically, speaking we can then say, *"The first female God created was not Eve but the planet Earth."* This maybe why some members of the New Age movement (of which I am definitely not) call the Earth, "Mother Earth." I understand and appreciate the fact that followers of Christ must be careful of being caught up in misguided New Age teachings that place man's ego and nature worship at the center of spirituality. However, Christians are acting like simpletons when we are afraid to acknowledge that some of the things members of the New Age say are actually true to the extent that "those things" confirm what the Bible actually teaches.

# ADAM & EVE

*And the Lord God formed man of the dust of the ground, and breathed into his nostrils the breath of life; and man became a living being. (Genesis 2:7)*

*Then the rib which the Lord God had taken from man He made into a woman, and He brought her to the man. And Adam said: "This is now bone of my bones and flesh of my flesh; She shall be called Woman because she was taken out of Man." (Genesis 2:22-23)*

Let us examine the above passages of Scripture. It's clearly evident that Adam (the male-man) was created first, making the male-man the first order of creation among humans. God gave this man complete dominion over planet Earth and the lower animal, maritime, insect and mineral kingdoms. However, something was missing. God said it this way; "It is not good for the man to be alone" (Genesis 2:18). What does this expression mean? Obviously, the man was not alone in a physical and spiritual sense because he was surrounded by the glory of God, angels and all the animals in the Garden of Eden. And yet we know that God cannot lie. So what does the statement, *"it is not good for the man to be alone"* mean? It means that even though the man was not lonely in a spiritual or physical sense, he was yet alone as a species. Adam had no way of generating his own species even though he was a walking warehouse of seed (sperm).

The question that quickly comes to my mind is simply this, "Who knows the Earth best, God or man?"

So what did God do to remedy the situation? He put the man to sleep while he performed surgery on the man. Interestingly enough, putting a patient to sleep during a surgery is standard practice in every surgery. God was the first surgeon to do so. Out of the man's rib, the

Lord formed the beautiful body of a compatible species, the female-man. When Adam came out of surgery and saw this beautiful compatible creature next to him, he was more than overjoyed. However, it's the language Adam used to describe Eve that is the focus of our study. And Adam said: *"This is now bone of my bones and flesh of my flesh; She shall be called Woman because she was taken out of Man."* Adam called this compatible creature "Woman." The word "Woman" is an interesting word. It references a Man with a womb or the womb-man. Most importantly the womb part of the woman was not spiritual but Earthly (fleshly). Since man's physical body is made of dirt or humus, it's safe to say that the Woman's ability to give birth or "bring forth" physical children is an extension of the Earth's womb. Just like the Earth beneath her feet, the woman needs a **seed** deposited in her womb in order to "bring forth!"

Women, like the Earth beneath, are incubators. If you sow wheat seeds in the womb of the Earth, expect a massive harvest of wheat, barring any drought. If you sow weed seeds in the womb of the Earth, expect a massive harvest of weeds. If you sow the seed of love in a woman, she will give you the harvest of a happy home. However, if you sow seeds of hate in a woman's life, expect a harvest of hell. Why? This is because both the Earth and women do not discriminate against the seed planted in their womb. The job of the Earth and woman's womb is to simply "bring forth a harvest of the **seed** sown." This similarity between the woman's and the Earth's womb is truly a fascinating bible study.

## MOTHER OF ALL THE LIVING

*And Adam called his wife's name Eve, because she was the mother of all living. (Genesis 3:20)*

After the fall, Adam named his wife Eve. The name Eve literally means "mother of all living beings (souls)." This name was very prophetic indeed because Eve had not yet given birth to children.

Adam's prophecy has been more than vindicated because all of today's living souls or beings came out of one woman, Eve.

## Mother Earth

If Eve is the mother of all living souls (persons) on this planet, and her physical body of dirt (henceforth her womb) came out of the Earth (dust of the ground), what does this say about the Earth itself? This question is of critical importance, especially if we are going to understand why we have to "speak to the Earth" to release prosperity. The planet Earth is the Mother of all living creatures and non-living physical substances. Look around you; do you see anything in the physical realm of matter, which did not originate from the Earth beneath your feet? I don't think you will find much.

Let us now examine "Mother Earth's" children.

   I.    Man's Physical Body (Genesis 2:7)
   II.   Wild Animals (Genesis 1:24)
   III.  Plants (Genesis 1:29)
   IV.   Trees (Genesis 1:12)
   V.    Grass (Genesis 1:12)
   VI.   Fish  (Genesis 1:21)
   VII.  Reptiles (Genesis 1:25)
   VIII. Birds (Genesis 1:21)
   IX.   Minerals (Genesis 2:11)
   X.    Cars
   XI.   Planes
   XII.  Machines
   XIII. Clothes
   XIV.  Shoes
   XV.   Houses

The fact that God treats the Earth as a "she" (the feminine article) explains the reason God and the Bible use the same descriptive terms to describe the Earth as they do a woman. For instance, the term "barren" is used to describe the Earth as well as a woman who cannot bring forth children. Take a look at the following Scriptures.

> *Then the men of the city said to Elisha, "Please notice, the situation of this city is pleasant, as my lord sees; but the water is bad, and the ground barren." (2 Kings 2:19)*

> *But they had no child, because Elizabeth was barren, and they were both well advanced in years. (Luke 1:7)*

As we come to the end of this chapter I want to focus on a foundational principle that the Holy Spirit gave me about the Earth that is extremely important. The Spirit of God said to me, "Francis, always remember, *"The EARTH is a SHE who can give birth to your blessings but Her mouth can also swallow your problems."*

## EARTH'S WOMB CAN GIVE BIRTH TO YOUR BLESSINGS!

*Then Isaac sowed in that land, and reaped in the same year a hundredfold; and the Lord blessed him. (Genesis 26:12)*

We have already proven through Scripture that Mother Earth's womb gave birth to man's physical body through the supernatural power of God. Her womb also gave birth to wild animals, birds, reptiles, fish and fruit trees and so forth. This begs the question, "What other goodies has God hidden in the womb of the Earth?" I believe the possibilities are boundless. It all depends on the creative ideas men and women receive from God in order to cause the womb of the Earth to bring forth what God has already deposited inside of it. The testimony of Scripture is clear, *"If we are willing and obedient, we shall eat the good of the land."* This Scripture implies that there is good or goodies that God has already deposited in the land (Earth) for us to enjoy.

> *If you are willing and obedient, you shall eat the good of the land; (Isaiah 1:19)*

Imagine this: for centuries, our forefathers were walking on foot or riding donkeys for hundreds of miles. Unbeknownst to them, the Earth beneath their feet was pregnant with automobiles and planes that could travel much faster than donkeys. All the raw materials needed to create automobiles or planes were buried in the womb of the Earth beneath their feet. All the oil or natural gas the automobiles, trains and planes would need as fuel was also buried in the womb of the Earth beneath their feet. All our ancestors lacked was a "divine revelation" or "seed thought" that would cause the Earth beneath their feet to bring forth out of its God given bounty.

"Woman" is an interesting word. It means a man with a womb or the womb-man."

## THE EARTH'S MOUTH CAN SWALLOW YOUR PROBLEMS!

If you remember in chapter one of this book, I mentioned how I almost died in the republic of Zambia. Things turned around in my favor when the Lord told me to pick up some dirt from the soil of Zambia and speak to the dirt. However, the last instruction God gave me baffled me. *"Now put back the soil in your hand into the Earth beneath your feet and I will bury those who tried to bury you."* The Spirit of God declared authoritatively. So I sought the Lord to show me what He meant by this militant statement. Since God is never afraid to back up everything He does with His Word, I knew that the answer would be forthcoming. When the answer came, it shook me and excited me at the same time. The answer came because of a question I asked the Lord: *"Lord, if speaking to the Earth is an ancient spiritual technology of the kingdom of God, who else did you reveal it to in the Bible?* To me this question was just the natural outflow of what God was revealing to me. I knew that God was not asking me to do something without biblical precedence.

## Dead Men Walking

*And Moses said, Hereby ye shall know that the Lord hath sent me to do all these works; for I have not done them of mine own mind. If these men die the common death of all men, or if they be visited after the visitation of all men; then the Lord hath not sent me. (Numbers 16:28-29)*

The Lord showed me that what He was teaching me about speaking to the Earth; He had already taught it to Moses, the servant of God. A spirit of insurrection came upon the sons of Korah as the children of Israel moved towards the Promise Land. The sons of Korah created what amounted to mutiny in the ranks of the people of Israel. They began to compete with Moses' leadership. They began to see Moses as a self-appointed leader, who could be easily challenged. So, they openly and publicly challenged him for the reins of leadership. Moses was very upset by their act of open rebellion, so much so that he cried to the Lord about it.

The moment Moses began to cry to God was the beginning of the end for the sons of Korah. They did not know that they had just become "dead men walking." The sentence of death was already upon their foreheads. In dishing out their judgment, Moses made a very interesting statement, *"If these men die the common death of all men, or if they be visited after the visitation of all men; then the Lord hath not sent me."* In essence, Moses was saying that if the sons of Korah died a natural death, then the Lord had not sent him to be an apostle to the Jewish people he took out of Egypt.

## EARTH: SWALLOW MY PROBLEMS

*But if the Lord make a new thing, and the earth open her mouth, and swallow them up, with all that appertain unto them, and they go down quick into the pit; then ye shall understand that these men have provoked the Lord. And it came to pass, as he had made an end of speaking all these words, that the ground clave asunder that was under them: (Numbers 16:30-31)*

Without a shadow of a doubt, the sons of Korah had become a real problem for Moses. There was great division and strife in the camp because of their actions. What immediately caught my attention is the portion in the biblical text where Moses, the man of God, begins to talk to the Earth. Just as God did in Genesis 4, Moses addressed the Earth as a "she" (her). This begs the question, "Who told him that the Earth was a "she" and that "she" had a mouth?"

Moses' description of Mother Earth is the exact same description of the Earth we find in Genesis chapter four when God was talking with Cain. Moses was not even alive when this conversation took place between God and Cain. However, since it was Moses who wrote the entire book of Genesis by divine revelation, I believe he saw by revelation God speak to the Earth in Genesis 1:11. By observing what the God of creation was doing, Moses realized that you can actually speak to the Earth to either cause it to bring forth or swallow.

The sons of Korah created a mutiny in the ranks of the people of Israel.

What is of note here is that Moses did not speak directly to angels or address God per se; instead he spoke directly to the Earth. He was very specific about what he told the Earth to do and how to do it. Functioning in the spirit of faith and Kingdom authority, Moses told the Earth beneath his feet to open up her "mouth" and swallow the sons of Korah. When it responded to the command of the man of God, the Earth also swallowed everything that belonged to the sons of Korah, including their property. Moses wanted no memory of them to remain in Israel. *Why would Moses speak to the Earth if he did not believe that it (Earth) had the God-given capacity to hear his faith-filled command?* As I stated earlier, it would be stupid of anybody to speak to an object that is incapable of hearing or responding. Moses asked the Earth" to open up her "mouth" and swallow all of Moses' problems. In this case, Moses' problems consisted of the sons of Korah and their camp of rebels. At the end of this book in the chapter on the prayer of activation, I will show you how you can also command the Earth to swallow problems in your life that are threatening to overwhelm and destroy your God-given destiny.

## THE EARTH'S RAPID RESPONSE

*And the earth opened her mouth and swallowed them up, and their houses, and all the men that appertained unto Korah, and all their goods. They, and all that appertained to them went down alive into the pit, and the earth closed upon them: and they perished from among the congregation. And all Israel that were round about them fled at the cry of them: for they said, Lest the earth swallow us up also. (Numbers 16:32-34)*

We have already stated in an earlier chapter that the *proof of hearing is response.* Not just any response but a response that is specific to what was requested. When we are able to harvest such a definitive response, it means that whatever object or entity we spoke to heard exactly what we said. This is truly mind-boggling! In Moses' case, we would expect to see the Earth open up her "mouth" and swallow all the sons of Korah, their descendants and their physical property, without infringing upon people who were innocent. *If speaking to the Earth is a precise technology of the Kingdom for manifesting dominion it can have no collateral damage.*

So what happened? To the people's utter dismay, they saw something they had never seen before. They saw the Earth beneath their feet open up her "mouth" and swallow the sons of Korah, their descendants and all of their property, without swallowing one innocent person! According to the Bible, the Earth swallowed about twenty three thousand people! That is a lot of people and a whole lot of problems that Moses did not have to contend with anymore.

I am not suggesting that you command the Earth to swallow your enemies (people you don't get along with). We are now under the new covenant of grace and the death of the Lord Jesus Christ on the cross mitigates how we use this powerful ancient spiritual technology and weapon of war. However, you should never hesitate to use this powerful tool to command the Earth to begin to swallow problems (demonic encroachments) that Satan has unleashed against you to try to drown your God-given destiny. It is my prayer that the Lord will cause the Earth beneath your feet to open her "mouth" to swallow all diabolical ploys, plots, maneuvers and subversive activities of Satan against your life, in Jesus' name I pray.

# LIFE APPLICATION SECTION
# MEMORY VERSES

*And the earth opened her mouth and swallowed them up, and their houses, and all the men that appertained unto Korah, and all their goods. They, and all that appertained to them went down alive into the pit, and the earth closed upon them: and they perished from among the congregation. And all Israel that were round about them fled at the cry of them: for they said, Lest the earth swallow us up also. (Numbers 16:32-34)*

# REFLECTIONS

1. How did Moses deal with the rebellion of the sons of Korah?

_____

_____

_____

_____

_____

_____

2. Why did Moses call the Earth a She?

_____

_____

_____

_____

_____

_____

# 8

# Redeeming the Land

*When I shut up heaven and there is no rain, or command the locusts to devour the land, or send pestilence among My people, if My people who are called by My name will humble themselves, and pray and seek My face, and turn from their wicked ways, then I will hear from heaven, and will forgive their sin and heal their land. (2 Chronicles 7:13-14)*

I HOPE AND PRAY that what I have already shared with you in this book has more than convinced you that there is a direct correlation between the spiritual world and the natural condition of the land. In the first chapter, I stated the fact that the land (Earth) is always the first witness when something is broken between God and man. This is why, before the Bible was written, God, in His eternal wisdom and mercy, used the condition of the land to show His people (Israel) His divine approval or disapproval.

In the above passage of Scripture, God gives King Solomon a divine template for "Healing or Redeeming the Land." This is a template for healing the land that has stood the test of time. Here is how it works: God told Solomon the tale-tale signs to look for when there is a curse operating on the land:

i.)  *If there is no open heaven;*

ii.)  *When there is no rain (drought);*

iii.) *Locusts (pests or parasites) that devour crops on the land;*

iv.) *Killer plagues (like Ebola or Cholera) breaking out on the population;*

v.)  *Unprecedented natural disasters like storms or earthquakes devastating the land.*

Using the 2 Chronicles 7:13-14 "model" for *redeeming the land,* God makes it adamantly clear that when you see the aforementioned tale-tale signs, there is something wrong spiritually between God and the country of the people in which these signs are appearing. However, this apostolic model also carries the remedy for healing the land. The remedy has several key triggers that I want to examine here, briefly.

## TRIGGER #1. IF MY PEOPLE

The first trigger to this apostolic model for healing the land is crystallized in the statement "If My people." This statement means that heathens (non-believers) in any country (nation) can *never initiate the healing of the land from spiritual ills that are affecting the land adversely.* The process of "healing the land" always starts with the Spirit of God laying a burden for the healing of the land on the hearts of God's covenant people. It takes a prophetic company of people who are spiritually connected to God to initiate the healing of the land. This is because the things of the "spirit world" are foolishness to the carnal mind. Most importantly, the unregenerate soul of man can never ever submit to God long enough to initiate real change in the spiritual climate of the land.

## TRIGGER #2. WHO ARE CALLED BY MY NAME

The second trigger to the apostolic model for healing the land is crystallized in the statement "Who are called by My name." This statement goes a step further and defines who among God's people can actually command an audience with God to initiate the healing of the land. The expression "who are called by My name" is referencing believers who are not just "talking the talk" but are actually "walking the walk!" God's name is His divine nature and character. So the expression "Who are called by My name" is calling for followers of Christ who have a proven testimony of manifesting the character and nature of God. This means that carnal Christians who are living for themselves lack standing before the presence of God and demonic powers to ask for the healing of the land. *How can we punish the works of disobedience on the land when our own obedience to God has not yet been fulfilled* (2 Corinthians 10:6)? Satan, (the accuser of the brethren), has legal standing before the Courts of Heaven to resist our petition for the healing of the land if our lifestyle is not different from that of the people who are "defiling the land."

## TRIGGER #3. WILL HUMBLE THEMSELVES

The third trigger to the apostolic model for healing the land is crystallized in the statement "will humble themselves." This statement compels us to move in the opposite direction to the spirit that works in the children of disobedience (Ephesians 2), which is the spirit of pride. Pride is the main reason unregenerate men fight against the will and counsel of God. It is this prideful resistance to God's word that ultimately leads them to violate God's holiness and open doors for demons to enter and defile the land. This is why God will not tolerate pride in His people who are praying for the healing of the land. *How can we function in the same spirit that led to the defilement of the land in the first place and expect to have legal standing to petition the Courts of Heaven for the healing of the land? The Scriptures are quite clear; God resists the proud but gives grace to the humble (James 4:6).*

## TRIGGER #4. AND PRAY

The fourth trigger to the apostolic model for healing the land is crystallized in the statement "and pray." This statement introduces us to the vehicle God always uses to communicate His heart, will and intent - prayer. *Prayer is the inescapable reality of living in the Kingdom of God.* There is no getting around the subject and activity of prayer if we hope to be successful with God. Church and revival history both testify to the fact that every time God has ever healed "barren land" or moved miraculously in any territory, the prevailing prayer of the saints in that region preceded the move of God. *Therefore I exhort first of all that supplications, prayers, intercessions, and giving of thanks be made for all men, for kings and all who are in authority, that we may lead a quiet and peaceable life in all godliness and reverence (1 Tim 2:1-2).*

There is a direct correlation between the spiritual world and the spiritual condition of the land.

## TRIGGER #5. AND SEEK MY FACE

The fifth trigger to the apostolic model for healing the land is crystallized in the statement "and seek My face." This statement immediately conveys two meanings; firstly, the expression "and seek My face" pinpoints the importance of seeking the will of God in the process of asking for the healing of the land. God has a specific will and plan for each territory; e.g. each state or country has a divine mandate it was called to fulfill. Please remember that nations and borders are God's brainchild. *And He has made from one blood every nation of men to dwell on all the face of the Earth, and has determined their pre-appointed times and the boundaries of their dwellings, so that they should seek the Lord, in the hope that they might grope for Him and find Him, though He is not far from each one of us. ( Acts 17:26-27).* The expression "And seek My face" then becomes the rallying cry for how we can heal the land by restoring it to its God-ordained calling and divine mandate.

Secondly, the expression "and seek My face" pinpoints the "attitude" that God requires in the hearts of the people who are praying for the healing of the land. Those who desire the heavenly kingdom to take them seriously must approach His majestic throne with a heart that hungers more for His presence than His acts. Many in the Body of Christ can't move certain mountains because they are too focused on His hands (what He can give them) while ignoring His face (which speaks of intimacy and fellowship). Please remember, the most fertile land without the presence of God is still accursed. We must, therefore, determine in our hearts to seek His face and not His hands as we cry out to Him to forgive our sin and heal our land.

## TRIGGER #6. AND TURN FROM THEIR WICKED WAYS

The final trigger to the apostolic model for healing the land is crystalized in the statement *"and turn from their wicked ways."* This statement introduces us to the most redemptive principle for redeeming souls and healing the land - repentance. *In the Kingdom of God, nothing starts over without repentance.* Repentance is more than the feeling of being sorry that you got caught; it's a state of mind. Repentance involves the act of changing one's mind in order to agree with God so you can move in the opposite direction, away from the behavior you are repenting about. The word <u>repentance</u> is actually made up of two very powerful English words, "Return" and "Penthouse". Repentance means: to "return" to the "penthouse." In every high-rise building, the penthouse is always found on the top of the building. *So repentance means to go back to the top of Kingdom living.*

Since there is nothing higher than God or His Kingdom and righteousness, repentance means to go back to God, His Kingdom and His righteousness. When a person is truly repentant, God is restored to His rightful position in that person's life. God's Kingdom is celebrated above any other and His righteousness (character) becomes the supreme desire of the person who has just gone through repentance.

The expression *"And turn from their wicked ways"* also gives us insight into what defiles the land - sin (wickedness)! The Bible tells us that sin is a reproach to any nation. *Righteousness exalteth a nation: but sin is a reproach to any people (Proverbs 14:34)*. We must come before God and repent for the sins of the nation and then cry out to God for the healing of the land. *We have sinned, and have committed iniquity, and have done wickedly, and have rebelled, even by departing from thy precepts and from thy judgments: Neither have we hearkened unto thy servants the prophets, which spake in thy name to our kings, our princes, and our fathers, and to all the people of the land (Daniel 9:5-6).*

## #7. THE RESULTS OF THE REMEDY

There is a world of difference between the living God that we are called to serve and idols carved by men's hands. *As for idols, they have eyes but do not see, they have ears but do not hear, they have hands but cannot touch, they have mouths but cannot speak, and they have legs but cannot walk.* Such is not the case with our God; He is a living God. If we do exactly as He has ordered or prescribed for us, He will never disappoint us. The aforementioned apostolic model from 2 Chronicles 7:13-14 guarantees us real results if we follow this divine prescription for the healing of the land. Let us quickly examine the results of following through with this prescription:

Prayer is the inescapable reality of living in the Kingdom of God.

### i) *Then I will hear from heaven*

The first result is crystallized in the statement, *"Then I will hear from heaven."* This expression means that the healing of the land always begins with God hearing our cry for deliverance. However, this is more than a casual acknowledgment of having heard someone talk or pray. This is the kind of hearing that moves God into positive action on behalf of His people. When God heard the cry of the children of Israel in Egypt (Exodus 3), He sent Moses to deliver them from their bondage. *This is the same kind of hearing that God promises here.*

### ii) And will forgive their sin

The second result is crystallized in the statement, *"And will forgive their sin."* This second result is extremely important in restoring the broken fellowship between God and His people. When it comes to the whole process of healing the land, this expression is also important in removing the sins of the nation from before the Lord. We all know that sin is what brings a reproach on any nation. Until it is repented from, the land can never experience real revival or lasting peace. The forgiving of sin also implies the removal of every consequence brought on the land by the sin of its people. *When Jesus saw their faith, He said to the paralytic, "Son, your sins are forgiven you." And some of the scribes were sitting there and reasoning in their hearts, "Why does this Man speak blasphemies like this? Who can forgive sins but God alone?" (Mark 2:5-7)* The Scriptures make it clear that only God can forgive sin. This also means that once God forgives sin, no man or demon can use it against us. It is as though it never happened.

### iii) And heal their land

The final result is crystallized in the statement, *"And heal their land."* This expression really excites me because of its far-reaching spiritual implication. The expression *"And heal their land"* makes it abundantly clear that God can heal "our land" as easily as He can heal the ails of individuals. This expression also betrays God's own passion for the corporate destiny of His people or entire regions.

I have no doubt that God wants to heal the land and peoples of the United States of America. However, He also wants to heal Nigeria, South Africa, Zimbabwe, Zambia, Australia, Europe and so forth. God can heal the land anywhere where He can gather a prophetic company of praying and worshipping warriors. Will you become one of those prayer warriors? Will you speak to the Earth in faith to release prosperity? *Then the men of the city said to Elisha, "Please notice, the situation of this city is pleasant, as my lord sees; but the water is bad, and the ground barren." And he said, "Bring me a new bowl, and put salt in it." So they brought it to him. Then he went out to the source of the water, and cast in the salt there, and said, "Thus says the Lord: 'I have healed this water; from it there shall be no more death or barrenness.'" So the water remains healed to this day, according to the word of Elisha which he spoke. (2 Kings 2:19-22)*

Sin is what brings a reproach on any nation and until it is forgiven, the land can never experience real revival.

## THE BLOOD CRIES OUT!

*And he said, what hast thou done? The voice of thy brother's blood crieth unto me from the ground. (Genesis 4:10)*

God asked Cain a question worth repeating once more, "What have you done?" This question tells us a lot about God and gives us *a prerequisite redeeming principle* for "healing the land." The question God asked Cain tells us implicitly that God never initiates the healing process until mankind takes responsibility for what we have done. This is why Daniel (Daniel 9) took the sins of his people upon his shoulders when he cried to God for the restoration of the Jewish people back to their homeland. This same question "What have you done?" was also addressed to Adam and Eve when they fell from their exalted position of dominion in the Garden of Eden: *"And the Lord God said to the woman, "What is this you have done?" (Genesis 3:13)*

Before Cain could answer, the Lord made another very important statement, which gives us yet another redeeming principle for "healing the land." *"The voice of thy brother's blood crieth unto me from the ground,"* the Lord declared. It's the first time in Scripture we are told that blood carries a distinctive "sound frequency" unique to the individual whose blood it is. Here is the redeeming principle: *"Whenever innocent blood is shed on Earth and mixes with the ground, both the blood and the land enjoin in a deafening cry for justice!"* This means that the shedding of innocent blood (such as the aborting of innocent unborn babies) drastically affects the prosperity and spiritual climate of the land. *So you shall not pollute the land in which you are; for blood pollutes the land, and no expiation can be made for the land for the blood that is shed on it, except by the blood of him who shed it. (Numbers 35:33)* Fortunately for us, the shed blood of Jesus Christ on the Cross-has a higher and lasting claim on the land. Jesus' blood has a higher claim on the land than the shed blood of innocents provided it's applied by faith in heartfelt repentance by God's people for the sins of the land.

## CURSED FROM THE EARTH!

*And now art thou cursed from the Earth, which hath opened her mouth to receive thy brother's blood from thy hand; (Genesis 4:11)*

This divine interaction between Cain and the Almighty God is loaded with redeeming or prerequisite principles for redeeming the land and breaking lingering curses over a region. In this particular instant, God establishes an immutable and universal "punitive principle" when He boldly declares, *"And now art thou cursed from the Earth, which hath opened her mouth to receive thy brother's blood from thy hand."* God establishes a punitive principle for which there is no door of escape outside of heartfelt repentance and applying the shed blood of Jesus which is the only blood in our universe that transcends and satisfies the cry for justice of any other shed blood *(to Jesus the Mediator of the new covenant, and to the blood of sprinkling that speaks better things than that of Abel. Hebrews 12:24).* In most law-abiding nations, the punitive principle that God attached to the shedding of innocent blood usually results in either a death or life-long prison sentence. This ancient punitive principle is an integral part of the penal code of all law-abiding nations.

> *When thou tillest the ground, it shall not henceforth yield unto thee her strength; a fugitive and a vagabond shalt thou be in the Earth. Genesis 4:12*

What got my attention when I was studying through this passage of Scripture in light of what happened to me in Zambia was the phrase *"And now art thou cursed from the Earth!"* The Holy Spirit immediately had me take note of this important fact. "The Curse" that came upon Cain for what he did, never came from God, or Heaven. The curse came from the "Earth" beneath his feet. The LORD showed me that a "curse" could either be on the land itself or come directly from the Earth (land) against someone, a family or a people group. Growing up in Africa I know for a fact that stories were told were a witch took some "dirt" in her hands cursed it and threw it against the building of a thriving business and the business suddenly went into bankruptcy. Usually great misfortunes befell its owners. I had never seen this in the Bible before until my time of warfare in the Republic of Zambia! God's people are truly being destroyed for the lack of knowledge (Hosea 4:6).

God never initiates the healing process until man takes responsibility for what he or she has done

## EARTH: CONTROLS SEEDTIME AND HARVEST

*While the **earth** remaineth, seedtime and harvest, and cold and heat, and summer and winter, and day and night shall not cease. (Genesis 8:22)*

One of the reasons we must definitely pray for the "healing of the land" is because God gave the Earth the power to control natural "Seedtime and Harvest." When you go to buy rice, vegetables, peanuts or cooking oil, you must realize that these things did not drop from heaven in their finished state. All of these essential items once existed in seed form inside the womb of the Earth. This is God's order of things. A farmer took the seed and planted it into the soil (Earth) hoping for a harvest (Genesis 8:22).

Before any farmer can have a harvest, the ground (Earth) must first use its womb to work on the seed sown. Barren land is land (Earth) that has lost its ability to properly process the seed and carry it to full term. I have seen looks of utter despair and devastation in countries where all the food crops failed. Everyone knows that if the land does not produce crops, starvation will quickly set it in. Whether we like it or not, "while the Earth remains, seedtime and harvest will never cease" and our personal or national prosperity is tied to the fertility or lack thereof of the land. This is why I love this spiritual technology of speaking to the Earth to release prosperity. Our God of abundance has loaded the womb of the Earth with every natural resource that you and I would ever need to fulfill our God-given destiny.

# LIFE APPLICATION SECTION
## MEMORY VERSES

*When I shut up heaven and there is no rain, or command the locusts to devour the land, or send pestilence among My people, if My people who are called by My name will humble themselves, and pray and seek My face, and turn from their wicked ways, then I will hear from heaven, and will forgive their sin and heal their land. (2 Chronicles 7:13-14)*

# REFLECTIONS

1. What are some of the prerequisites before God heals the land?

_____
_____
_____
_____
_____

2. What was the blood of Abel doing?

_____
_____
_____
_____
_____

# 9

# Jesus Redeems the Earth

*Now I saw a new heaven and a new earth, for the first heaven and the first earth, had passed away. Also, there was no more sea. (Revelation 21:1)*

IT IS QUITE clear from observing the above passage of Scripture that Heaven and Earth have and will always be a part of God's master plan for mankind. The writer of the book of Revelation demonstrates in the above passage of Scripture that God does not intend to abandon the only life-sustaining planet in the entire universe - Earth. In creating a new heaven and a new Earth, God is showing us the importance of the planet we live on. When the devil, demons and all fallen angels have been cast into the lake of fire and brimstone, planet Earth will continue to remain. This being the case, it is no wonder Jesus had to redeem the Earth before He even went to the cross.

## THORNS AND THISTLES

*Then to Adam He said, "Because you have heeded the voice of your wife, and have eaten from the tree of which I*

*commanded you, saying, 'You shall not eat of it': "Cursed*
*is the ground for your sake; In toil you shall eat of it all the*
*days of your life. Both thorns and thistles it shall bring*
*forth for you, and you shall eat the herb of the field. (Genesis*
*3:17-18)*

We all know that the fall of man in the Garden of Eden was
catastrophic. When Adam and Eve, the first Kingdom ambassadors
fell into temptation and committed high treason against the
Sovereign God, everything went into a tailspin. The first visible sign
that things in the Garden of Eden and in the world would never be the
same again was evidenced by the negative reaction from the
ground (Earth) beneath their feet. God told Adam that because
he had decided to listen to the voice of his wife instead of what
God had told him, the land beneath his feet would be under a curse.
This curse would operate in three major ways:

### i) *In toil you shall eat of it all the days of your life.*

The first order of this curse is crystallized in the statement, *"In toil*
*you shall eat of it all the days of your life."* This statement means that
the fall of Adam and Eve drastically changed man's initial disposition
towards the Earth. Instead of the Earth heeding man's voice to "bring
forth," the Earth would contend with man's voice. This contention or
refusal to obey man's command from the ground beneath would create
a spiritual and natural condition called "toil." The word "toil" is
defined as *hard and continuous work; exhausting labor or effort.*
Quick examination of the working conditions in the Garden of Eden
before the fall of man will reveal that Adam's work was a refreshing
flow of divine favor. Adam and Eve were strangers to a life of
exhausting labor. This is why people who are sentenced to long prison
sentences with hard labor wither away very quickly. I hope you are
starting to appreciate why the Lord Jesus had to redeem the Earth
from the curse that came upon it after the fall of Adam and Eve.

 In creating a new heaven and a new Earth, God is showing us the importance of the planet we live on.

### ii)  Both thorns and thistles it shall bring forth for you

The second order of this "curse" is crystallized in the statement, "Both thorns and thistles it shall it bring forth for you." Instead of the luscious green that paraded the Garden of Eden, mankind was introduced to an Earthly environment forged in hostility against his very well being. Having grown up in Africa, I can tell you with certainty that trying to cultivate a piece of land that is full of thorns and thistles is a living hell. The first thing you have to do to make the piece of land conducive for cultivation is spend hours clearing the land of thorns and thistles. If you plant seeds in soil that is full of thorns and thistles, the thorns and thistles will eventually overwhelm the germinated plants and choke the budding plants. Without a doubt, it was never God's intention for the Earth to bring forth thorns and thistles.

## DON'T SWEAT IT!

*In the sweat of your face, you shall eat bread, till you return to the ground, for out of it you were taken; for dust you are, and to dust you shall return. (Genesis 3:19)*

### iii)  In the sweat of your face, you shall eat bread

Have you heard the expressions, "Don't sweat it or don't sweat the small things?" I am sure many of you have heard people say this to people who are under undue distress. The commonality between the two statements is the underlying beliefs that "sweat" is the proof that we are functioning out of divine alignment. What is of note here is that "sweat" is a foreign and demonic condition that was introduced to mankind as a spiritual consequence of man's disobedience to God's Word and sovereign authority. So "sweating" is an integral part of the curse.

What makes "sweat" a big issue as related to our study in this book is the "spiritual connection" between "sweat" and the Earth. According to God, the curse that came upon the ground (land/Earth) would manifest itself in such a way that the Earth would forcefully resist man's efforts to harvest from the ground beneath until man's body breaks out into a "sweat." This means that "sweat" is a sure sign that we are failing to dominate what God ordained for us to dominate. God never intended for man to struggle to cause the Earth to bring forth.

## GOD HATES BARRENNESS

*"I am the true vine, and My Father is the vinedresser. Every branch in Me that does not bear fruit He takes away; and every branch that bears fruit He prunes, that it may bear more fruit. (John 15:1-2)*

It is difficult to look at the above passage of Scripture without coming up with the conclusion that God hates all forms of barrenness. When Jesus makes the statement, *"Every branch in Me that does not bear fruit He takes away;"* He's making it very clear that God the Father expects "fruit" from everyone and everything in creation that bears the fingerprint of God. In the marketplace, bearing fruit is the difference between running your business into the ground or succeeding in a big way.

In the world of business bearing fruit is the equivalent of producing profit-bearing results. Without fruit or profit producing results, all we're doing is spinning our wheels while going nowhere. If we extrapolate this principle and apply it to the Earth, the Earth producing fruit is tantamount to the Earth manifesting in "time" everything God intended for this planet. This is why *speaking to the Earth*, which is the subject of this book, is very important. When we speak or prophesy to the Earth, we are causing it to bring forth by faith what we need in order to advance the Kingdom of God.

> *Then the men of the city said to Elisha, "Please notice, the situation of this city is pleasant, as my lord sees; but the water is bad, and the ground barren." And he said, "Bring me a new bowl, and put salt in it." So they brought it to him. Then he went out to the source of the water, and cast in the salt there, and said, "Thus says the Lord: 'I have healed this water; from it there shall be no more death or barrenness.'" So the water remains healed to this day, according to the word of Elisha, which he spoke. (2 Kings 2:19-22)*

In my humble opinion, there are very few Scriptures in the Bible that capture the spirit of the book you are now holding in your hands like the above passage of Scripture. This passage of Scripture shows us why God wants us to remember that He gave us the power to speak to the Earth to bring forth life instead of death. Immediately after the mantle of the prophet Elijah was transferred to Elisha, city leaders came to him with a matter of grave concern. They told him that the outside of the city looked good to tourists but internally, the city had some very serious challenges. They told him that the water in the city was polluted and the land itself was barren.

**Without a doubt, it was never God's intention for the Earth to bring forth thorns and thistles.**

Interestingly enough, Elisha did not get upset with them for bringing him a citywide problem that in the natural was better suited to be handled by scientists, geologists and chemical engineers. Elisha knew that as a man of God, he carried within his mantle the ability to "Speak to the Earth" and cause it to bring forth what was needed to sustain the livelihood of the populace. The thing that really captured my attention is the tool that the prophet used to heal the polluted waterways and the barren land. He used *"salt and the spoken Word!"* These tools became the architects of the transformation that the city soon experienced. What's more, these powerful spiritual tools are also available to New Testament believers in Christ.

## YOU ARE THE SALT OF THE EARTH

*"You are the salt of the Earth; but if the salt loses its flavor, how shall it be seasoned? It is then good for nothing but to be thrown out and trampled underfoot by men. (Matthew 5:13)*

When the prophet Elisha healed the polluted waters of the city and its barren land, he used salt and the spoken Word. Centuries later, the Lord Jesus comes on the scene and gives us a deeper prophetic meaning of the "salt" that Elisha used to heal the city. Jesus looked at His disciples and made the statement, *"You are the salt of the Earth"* and then makes it clear that the purpose of "salt" is to give food its flavor. In this statement, "flavor" represents divine influence.

When you put salt in food, you influence how the food tastes. Consequentially when Jesus said, *"You are the salt of the Earth,"* He was in effecting saying that God's children have a gift and calling to influence the Earth with the power, principles and culture of the Kingdom of Heaven. If we lose our "saltiness" (influence), we are of no use to the Kingdom of God. When we speak to the Earth to bring forth righteousness, while binding the spirit of corruption, we are in effect influencing the Earth. We are in such cases acting as the "salt" of the Earth.

# JESUS' BLOOD REDEEMS THE EARTH

*Now an angel from heaven appeared to Him, strengthening Him. And being in agony, He was praying very fervently; and His sweat became like drops of blood, falling down upon the ground. (Luke 22:43-44)*

Before God gave me the revelation that birthed the book you are holding in your hands or reading on your device, it never dawned on me that the Earth (ground) *was the first recipient of the precious blood of our Savior.* The Earth beneath tasted the redeeming power of the blood of Jesus before mankind ever tasted the redeeming and life changing power of the blood of Jesus. When I finally saw this important fact in the canon of Scripture, I was blown away. What a God we serve!

Our God is such a God of purpose and divine order. In redeeming mankind, God went about it in a sequential order. Since the fall of Adam and Eve happened in a garden and drastically affected the fertility of the Earth, Jesus went into another garden (Gethsemane) and wrestled with the same old serpent that deceived the first Adam. In the Garden of Gethsemane, Jesus wrestled with the devil until **His will was fully aligned with God's will.** The battle was so intense that *"His sweat became like drops of blood,"* which fell down to the ground (Earth).

Ask yourself the question, *"How can the precious blood of Jesus fall to the ground and the ground remain cursed?"* It is not possible at all for the ground to remain cursed. This leads us to the logical conclusion that the blood of Jesus removed the "curse" that caused the ground to produce "thorns and thistles." It removed the curse of toil and sweat that changed man's dominion disposition towards the Earth. This means that ever since the blood of Jesus fell onto the ground, the Earth has been restored to its original position of "bringing forth" prosperity at man's command. This is why we can "speak to the Earth" with authority and expect it to bring forth the harvest of prosperity that the Lord prepared for us before the foundation of the world.

# YOU SHALL EAT THE GOOD OF THE LAND

*If you are willing and obedient, you shall eat the good of the land (Isaiah 1:19)*

The above passage of Scripture is one of my favorite Bible passages. God states two spiritual conditions that precede God-given prosperity: *"If you are willing and obedient."* These two conditions are intertwined at the hip by the "will of God." The first condition, "willingness" deals with our willingness to bend our will to God's will. The second condition, "obedience" measures our response to God's will in our visible response to what He tells us to do. If God says, "go right" and we go left, we have in effect demonstrated our inability to offer God the two conditions He needs to sanction our material prosperity on Earth; *our willingness and obedience.*

Without a doubt, it was never God's intention for the Earth to bring forth thorns and thistles.

However, if God says, "go right" and "we go right," we have in effect demonstrated our ability to offer God the two conditions He needs to sanction our material prosperity on Earth; *our willingness and obedience*. Once these two conditions are fully satisfied, God promises us our share of the good of the land. The expression, "the good of the land" infers the very best the land has to offer. In other words, if you live in a country that is known for having oil, precious minerals and other resources, having some of these things in your portfolio of investments is "eating from the good of the land." If we live a life of obedience, God will personally manifest our prosperity. This means that when "we speak to the Earth" to bring forth, it will quickly *bring forth in our favor!*

*When I have brought them to the land flowing with milk and
honey, of which I swore to their fathers, and they have eaten
and filled themselves and grown fat, then they will turn to
other gods and serve them; and they will provoke Me and
break My covenant. (Deuteronomy 31:20 NKJV)*

*"One of the best-recognized descriptions of the land of Israel is "a
land flowing with milk and honey (Deut. 31:20). This description
immediately conjures up a picture of a rich, fertile and desirable land
– but what do the words actually mean and what environmental
implications are alluded to in this expression?* We start with the
interpretation of the Talmud, which interprets the words zavat halav
u'dvash, (flowing with milk and honey) as milk flows from the goats'
(udders) and honey flows from the dates and the figs (Ketubot 111b).
For a pastoral people, this indeed must have been an inviting description
of the land. The goats were a source of milk as well as meat and were
very prolific. In biblical times, goats were a reflection of wealth." *(By
Rabbi Yuval Cherlow)*

Without a doubt Deuteronomy 31:20 forever establishes the
indispensable divine connection between prosperity and the good of
the land. This passage clearly suggests that if the land is poor or barren
of wealth generating natural resources, the inhabitants of the land
suffer the consequences thereof in their personal economy. This is
why, when God took the children of Israel out of Egypt, it was with
this promise: *"When I have brought them to the land flowing with milk
and honey, of which I swore to their fathers, and they have eaten and
filled themselves and grown fat, then they will turn to other gods and
serve them; and they will provoke Me and break My covenant."* When
the children of Israel finally arrived in the Promise Land, it was exactly
as God had promised them forty years earlier. *I believe that it's now
your time to enter your land of fulfilled destiny.* The Bible calls it a
land flowing with milk and honey. *Are you ready to "speak to the
Earth" and demand that it bring forth prosperity?* I surely hope so!

# LIFE APPLICATION SECTION
## MEMORY VERSES

*Now an angel from heaven appeared to Him, strengthening Him. And being in agony, He was praying very fervently; and His sweat became like drops of blood, falling down upon the ground. (Luke 22:43-44)*

# REFLECTIONS

1. What happened to the land when Jesus shed His blood in the Garden of Gethsemane?

_____

_____

_____

_____

_____

_____

2. What the two prerequisites God looks for to guarantee our prosperity?

_____

_____

_____

_____

_____

_____

# 10

# The Zimbabwe Miracle: The Healing of a Nation

*Ask of Me, and I will give You, the nations for Your inheritance, and the ends of the Earth for Your possession. (Psalm 2:8)*

In September 2014, God supernaturally opened a door for me to fly to Zimbabwe to attend the Synod Conference hosted by Tom Deuschle, Pastor of Celebration Church in Borrowdale, Harare. Harare is the capital city of Zimbabwe, a beautiful land-locked country that borders Zambia on the West and South Africa on the South. Zimbabwe, formerly known as Southern Rhodesia, got its independence from British colonial rule in 1980 through the sacrificial efforts of freedom fighters such as Robert Mugabe and Emmerson Mnangagwa. In 1980, the people of Zimbabwe celebrated their independence from British rule with great fanfare. They even invited the legendary reggae singer, Bob Marley, to perform in the newly independent country. Bob Marley composed a famous song about Zimbabwe, under a title bearing the country's name.

Unfortunately, for the people of Zimbabwe, their festive mood would slowly but surely morph into a tortured decline into the erasing of civil liberties, the rule of law, as well as a rapid descent into an economic abyss such as no other African country has ever known. *Where were the prognosticators or prophets of God during Zimbabwe's independence celebrations?* No one could have predicted that their conquering hero, Robert Mugabe, would become one of Africa's longest surviving dictators. His dictatorial rule would bring the nation's economy to a complete standstill. No one then would have predicted that 37 years later the entire nation of Zimbabwe would be demonstrating by the thousands in the streets of Harare demanding the immediate expulsion of their once conquering hero from the Presidency.

## THE BIRTH OF A DICTATOR

As soon as Robert Mugabe assumed power, he began to move away from any semblance of a functional democratic state. He quickly entrenched Zimbabwe's politics into a one-party state, which effectively meant he could rule the country without any real challenge from a rival politician from another political party. Then, he moved swiftly into exterminating any kind of dissent to his authoritarian rule. Some of his political enemies were killed under very suspicious circumstances. *The soil of Zimbabwe was stained with the blood of Mugabe's political enemies.* Then, he moved to expel white Zimbabwean farmers from their farms in order to give the land to his political cronies and henchmen. Some white farmers were killed and some of their women were even raped by Mugabe's political mobs. However, you wouldn't know it from watching the state run media, Zimbabwe News Corporation. They aired programs that showed the rest of the world a prospering Zimbabwe, completely removed from the realities on the ground.

Unfortunately, Mugabe's political cronies and mobs had no clue on how to run and manage a successful farming business. Farms that once flourished under the management of white Zimbabwean farmers were transformed into barren wastelands.

Soon a country that had been named the "bread basket of Africa" was experiencing critical food shortages.

## A STOLEN ELECTION

Everywhere in Zimbabwe, the mood had shifted into utter despondence with a mixture of hopeful optimism that the aging Mugabe would soon relinquish the reins of power following the footsteps set by the legendary Nelson Mandela, when he willingly gave up the reins of power over South Africa after one presidential term. Unfortunately, for the people of Zimbabwe, Robert Mugabe did not share Nelson Mandela's nobler qualities. Political power for Mugabe was a drug from which there existed no cure.

In 2013, when the first multi-party democratic elections were held in Zimbabwe, desperate citizens saw a way out of the chokehold Mugabe and his family had on a nation that was loaded with so much potential and promise. Zimbabweans overwhelmingly voted for Movement for Democratic Change (MDC) leader Morgan Tsvangirai. Morgan Tsvangirai was an upcoming and fiery charismatic leader . Election monitors from around the world clearly declared Morgan Tsvangirai the winner of the Presidential elections. However, Mugabe and his political cronies did not release the election results for weeks. They managed, through sheer public intimidation, to whip up some more votes, especially from the rural areas. They found a way for Mugabe to be declared the winner. For many Zimbabweans who had hoped this was the end of Mugabe's reign, the fraudulent election results were quite demoralizing.

## A BOTTOMLESS ECONOMIC PIT

Just when you thought things couldn't get any worse, they did. Zimbabwe's economy took a nosedive like a jumbo jet falling in flight having lost all of its engines. The inflation rate was astronomical to say the least. The inflation rate in Zimbabwe had no historical precedence. No country in human history had ever had it this bad. A piece of bread would cost millions of ZIM dollars which meant ordinary Zimbabweans would carry a bag full of ZIM dollars just to go and buy a piece of bread. Hundreds of thousands of Zimbabweans fled the country for greener pastures in neighboring countries such as South Africa, Zambia, Botswana and Kenya, just to name a few. Some institutional banks collapsed in the wake of the unchecked inflation. The business climate was toxic. The only way out of this economic abyss was to decommission Zimbabwe's currency and bring in the US dollar to stabilize an economy in free fall. This move temporarily stabilized the country's economy. I flew to Zimbabwe soon after this.

I quickly fell in love with the nation and people of Zimbabwe and my host church also received me very well. Soon my books, such as *The Order of Melchizedek and The Joseph of Arimathea Calling,* were being sold all over the nation of Zimbabwe. I started speaking for some of Zimbabwe's elite pastors and preachers. God quickly made it clear to me that even though I was born in Zambia and lived in the United States of America; He was making me an apostle to the nation of Zimbabwe. Soon after, even secular radio stations and the Zimbabwe Broadcasting Corporation were inviting me to speak to the nation of Zimbabwe. While visiting Zimbabwe, I also linked up with gospel giants such Bishop Tudor Bismarck who graciously gave me his apostolic blessing to minister in the nation of Zimbabwe.

## SPEAKING TO THE EARTH: SHIFTING THE SANDS OF TIME

November 5th, 2017, I took part in a Sunday evening service at Celebration Church in Borrowdale, Harare that I will never forget for as long as I live. *I was the special guest speaker for an evening Sunday worship service that quickly morphed into a sovereignly orchestrated intercessory prayer meeting for the healing of the nation of Zimbabwe.* Before the evening service, I met with two senior church leaders who wanted me to give them a debriefing of my Sunday evening message. I told them that the Lord had laid it upon my heart to speak on the revelation He had given me on "Speaking to the Earth!" *I told them that I felt that this tool of the Spirit would shift the sands of time in people's lives and also aid in redeeming the land of Zimbabwe from the iniquity that had defiled the land.* I got the blessing of these two leaders and Pastor Tom Deuschle to teach this revelation to their congregation. They made arrangements to collect soil from the church grounds and place it in buckets. This soil was what we used at the end of my message in the prophetic act of speaking to the Earth. After I finished teaching on how to "Speak to the Earth to Release Prosperity Over the Land," congregants came forward to take small amounts of the soil in their hands. I then led over 2,000 people who attended this life-changing service through the prophetic act of repenting for the iniquities that were imposed upon the land of Zimbabwe by its forefathers. *We then corporately rededicated the land of Zimbabwe to the Lord and the Lord urged me to challenge the people to pray for the birth of a "new Zimbabwe!"*

*If My people who are called by My name will humble themselves, and pray and seek My face, and turn from their wicked ways, then I will hear from heaven, and will forgive their sin and heal their land. (2 Chronicles 7:14)*

A spirit of prophetic intercession like I have never seen before fell on everybody who was there! I saw thousands of people praying with the intensity of one man. We prayed earnestly for the healing of the land of Zimbabwe. As we were interceding for the nation of Zimbabwe, I saw a "new Zimbabwe" coming through the birth canal. I began calling it out by the spirit of prophecy. We were all excited and energized by the Holy Spirit as we felt very strongly that God was giving us, His dear children, the power to re-negotiate the destiny of the nation of Zimbabwe in the Courts of Heaven.

## THE HEAVENLY VISION THAT CHANGED A NATION!

*Who has heard such a thing? Who has seen such things? Shall the Earth be made to give birth in one day? Or shall a nation be born at once? For as soon as Zion was in labor, She gave birth to her children. Shall I bring to the time of birth, and not cause delivery?" says the Lord. "Shall I who cause delivery shut up the womb?" says your God. (Isaiah 66:8-9)*

As long as I could remember, the above portion of Scripture has fascinated me. *How can a nation be born anew in one day?* Apart from the nation of Israel, which became a nation again in "one day" in 1948 by a decree of the United Nations, this kind of rapid shift in a nation's destiny is almost unheard of. Going forward, I personally have to include Zimbabwe in this conversation as a distant second. After we finished the prophetic act of "speaking to the soil of Zimbabwe" and commanding it to shift, I asked the people to come to the altar and put the soil back into the buckets. The people who attended that memorable Sunday evening service graciously did so. Suddenly, a spirit of worship fell upon us and we started worshipping the Lord. As we were worshipping the Lord, the Holy Spirit tugged on my heart to pick up one of the blue buckets containing the soil of Zimbabwe. I knelt down and picked up the blue bucket and began to wave it to the Lord as a "wave offering" while the worship team led us in an intimate time of worship. While I was waving the blue bucket of soil before the Lord, some of the pastoral staff at Celebration Church and some other church members joined me spontaneously in lifting the other blue buckets of soil to the Lord, as we waved the soil of Zimbabwe as an offering before the Lord. It was such a beautiful sight!

Suddenly, I had one of the most incredible heavenly visions I have ever had! I suddenly found myself in God's heavenly courtroom. I saw the Heavenly Father seated in judicial robes as the Righteous Judge. He took the soil of Zimbabwe from the blue buckets of soil and He put the soil inside a transparent glass that looked like an ancient hourglass. He then labeled it with the word "Zimbabwe." What happened next took my breath away! The Heavenly Father reached across His judicial bench and gave the hourglass containing the soil of Zimbabwe to the Lord Jesus who stood in His place of advocacy in the Courts of Heaven. The Heavenly Father smiled at Jesus, gave Him the hourglass containing the soil of Zimbabwe and said, "This nation now belongs to you!" That's how the vision, ended!

*By faith we understand that the worlds were framed by the word of God, so that the things, which are seen, were not made of things, which are visible. (Hebrews 11:3)*

I knew instantly, with tremendous conviction that the nation of Zimbabwe had shifted irreversibly in the realm of the spirit. Since the spirit world is the "causal realm," I knew that the results of what had happened in the Courts of Heaven would eventually manifest on the nation of Zimbabwe. I knew that the Earth beneath our feet had shifted significantly. I knew that the land of Zimbabwe would begin to self-correct and spew out those who were central to defiling the land! Monday morning, November 6th, 2017, the nation of Zimbabwe was shaken by Robert Mugabe's sudden dismissal of the nation's Vice-President Emmerson Mnangagwa, who was deeply beloved by the people of Zimbabwe. Mugabe made this irrational decision because he wanted to make way for his domineering wife, Grace "Gucci" Mugabe to become the Vice-President so she could then succeed Robert Mugabe as Zimbabwe's second president since its independence from Great Britain.

The Pastor who was driving me around was a bit concerned about the turn of events and I assured him that everything that would happen in Zimbabwe after the prophetic act of speaking to the Earth that we had done that Sunday night, would be the land of Zimbabwe, "self-correcting" itself back to righteous foundations. Apparently, the firing of Vice-President Emmerson Mnangagwa, was what triggered and unified the Zimbabwe Defense Forces to take action to end Robert Mugabe's dictatorial reign over the nation of Zimbabwe. The day after my apostolic team and I flew out of Zimbabwe is the day the Army took over the country and placed Mugabe under house arrest. The miracle of it all is that in Africa and other parts of the world, military coups of governments are soiled in blood. However when the Zimbabwe Defense Forces took temporal control of Zimbabwe, there was no bloodshed! Within days, millions of Zimbabweans were marching peacefully in the streets of Zimbabwe demanding the immediate resignation of President Robert Mugabe. I watched these historic events take place from the comfort of my home in America. I was stunned and awed by the greatness of our God as He freed His people in Zimbabwe from the tyrannical choke-hold of one man and his Jezebel wife.

I remembered prophesying to the people of Zimbabwe that the Lord told me that Zimbabwe would not regress back to the very difficult time it had in 2008, when its economy took a nosedive. I prophesied that a new Zimbabwe had been birthed and that the nation's destiny was fully secure. I prophesied that Zimbabwe would once again become "the bread basket of Africa" and foreign investments and aid would abound in the new Zimbabwe. *I watched with prayerful anticipation as a new nation rose slowly from the ashes of despair.* What a God we serve! It's my deepest prayer that the spiritual technology of "Speaking to the Earth" that is contained in this book would become a "working model" all over the world for the healing of the land. God is a God of nations and He is very interested in healing entire nations! Can a nation be born in one day? Yes it can!

# LIFE APPLICATION SECTION
## MEMORY VERSES

*Who has heard such a thing? Who has seen such things? Shall the Earth be made to give birth in one day? Or shall a nation be born at once? For as soon as Zion was in labor, She gave birth to her children. Shall I bring to the time of birth, and not cause delivery?" says the Lord. "Shall I who cause delivery shut up the womb?" says your God. (Isaiah 66:8-9)*

## REFLECTIONS

1. Why does God want to heal entire Nations?

_____

_____

_____

_____

_____

_____

2. How do you intend to use the revelation contained in this book to shift your region?

_____

_____

_____

_____

_____

_____

# 11

# ACTIVATION:
# Speaking to the Earth
# Prayer

*What does it profit, my brethren, if someone says he has faith but does not have works? Can faith save him? If a brother or sister is naked and destitute of daily food, and one of you says to them, "Depart in peace, be warmed and filled," but you do not give them the things which are needed for the body, what does it profit? Thus also faith by itself, if it does not have works, is dead. (James 2:14-17)*

THE ABOVE PASSAGE of Scripture is one of my favorite passages in the Bible. The reason? It makes faith become a practical matter. James, the apostle, poses a very powerful question, *"What does it profit, my brethren if someone says he has faith but does not have works?"* It is quite clear from the question he posed that James, the apostle, expects people of faith to profit spiritually from the usage of their faith. He also goes on to make it clear that *faith without works is dead*. This is why I believe that this chapter on the prayer of activation is probably one of the most important chapters in this entire book.

In this particular chapter, I will teach you how to activate in "real-time" this ancient spiritual technology of "Speaking to the Earth" *in order to cause it to bring forth! This spiritual technology is powerful enough to shift entire regions because it is rooted in the supernatural power of God.* However, we must not forget that the Word of God will profit us nothing if it is not mixed with faith *(For indeed the gospel was preached to us as well as to them; but the word which they heard did not profit them, not being mixed with faith in those who heard it. Hebrews 4:1).*

This was the problem of the children of Israel who came out of Egypt. Even though God had gloriously delivered and given them a sure word of promise, they nevertheless failed to enter the Promise Land. Thousands of years later, the writer of the book of Hebrews lets us know the reason they could not enter into the Promise Land: they did not mix the Word that God gave them with faith. It is my prayer that as you get ready to activate this powerful, ancient spiritual technology for manifesting kingdom dominion on planet Earth that you do so by faith. It is impossible to please God without faith!

## BEFORE YOU PRAY

I want to give you some practical tips before you use this prayer of activation. Before you start praying, I want you to make sure that you do the following:

1. *Find a quiet room in which to pray or preferably, you can pray outside your home, business or church.*

2. *Get a bucket and fill it with dirt. If you don't have a bucket, you can simply dip your hand into the soil and pick up some dirt.*

3. *Get rid of all distractions, such as cell phones before you begin to pray.*

4. *Speak out loud the prophetic activation prayer from this book and do so by faith.*

5. *Remember that without faith it is impossible to please God (Hebrews 11:6)*

## Prayer For Speaking To The Earth:

"Heavenly Father, I stand in Your royal and heavenly courtroom through the blood of Jesus and I ask that the Courts be seated according to Daniel 7:10. Heavenly Father, I have come to receive Your righteous judgment over my spiritual inheritance and destiny here on Earth. Heavenly Father, according to Psalm 103:20, I call upon Your holy angels to be supernatural enforcers of my righteous plea and also I summon the 24 elders (Revelation 5:14) to be witnesses to this legal and righteous transaction. I also decree and declare that all the demonic powers, whether they be principalities, powers or rulers of darkness that are subverting my prophetic destiny here on Earth will respect and honor Your righteous judgment over my spiritual inheritance here on Earth.

Heavenly Father, Your Word says, *"If we confess our sins, you are faithful and just to forgive our sin and cleanse us from all unrighteousness (1 John 1:9)."* Heavenly Father, forgive me for any ancestry or personal sin that has caused the Earth beneath my feet not to give me of its fullness. Heavenly Father, I choose to forgive every person who has ever hurt me even as You forgave me in Christ Jesus. Before I speak and command the Earth to shift in my favor, I let go of every root of bitterness in Jesus's name, I pray.

Heavenly Father, as I prepare to speak to the Earth, I denounce all illegal spiritual trades that I and my forefathers have ever made on Satan's trading floors in the second heaven that have given Satan the legal grounds to subvert my financial prosperity and the establishment of my destiny here on Earth. I repent for all violations of God's law and holiness that my ancestors and me created on Satan's trading floors. Heavenly Father, I petition Your royal and supreme Court to issue a decree releasing me from the spiritual consequences of every illegal spiritual transaction. I appeal to the precious blood of Jesus to wipe out everything Satan has on me in his prosecutorial records. Heavenly Father, in the name of the Lord

Jesus Christ, I repent on behalf of this Nation (name the name of the city or country you are in) for all the shedding of innocent blood, especially that of aborted babies. I decree and declare that I will not be a vagabond or a fugitive on Earth, like Cain who was cursed from the ground beneath. I decree and declare that the blood of Jesus Christ now sets me FREE to prosper in every area of my life here on Earth.

NOW I SAY….. (At this stage point one of your fingers towards the dirt in one of your hands)

Earth, Earth…hear the Word of the Lord! I stand before El Elyon (The Most High God), the possessor of heaven and Earth and Father of our Lord Jesus Christ. I call His holy angels to be witnesses and enforcers of this legal and righteousness transaction. It is written in Psalms 24:1 *that the earth is the Lord's and the fullness thereof, the world and they that dwell therein.* It is also written in Psalms 115:16 that *the heavens belong to the Lord but the earth, He has given to the children of men.* Heavenly Father, according to Your Word, You created the Earth and filled it with Your fullness so that everything that I would ever need to fulfill Your will for my life would be provided for me from the womb of the Earth.

Heavenly Father, it is also written in Your Word that You have given dominion over the Earth to the children of men (Genesis 1:26). So, in front of El Elyon (The Most High God) and the Lord Jesus Christ, I prophesy and take authority over the Earth that this country stands on. I say… "Earth, Earth: I command and charge you to open your mouth and vomit all the blessings that the Lord ordained for me to possess and enjoy from before the foundation of the world. I ask this in the mighty name of Jesus of Nazareth. Hear these words of mine, Earth, Earth….I release you this very moment from any demonic ploys, covenants, curses, hexes or witchcraft spells that you have been brought into by the children of wickedness.

As a highly exalted Ambassador of Christ and joint heir with Jesus, I release you Earth, Earth from the burden of having to obey the words of the children of wickedness. Earth, Earth…I decree and declare that you will no longer be subdued by the evil words of those who despise the name of the Lord and His glorious Kingdom. You are now legally and righteously relieved of your duty to the children of wickedness. I now employ you in the service of Christ and His Kingdom. Earth, Earth…hear the Word of the Lord. I now command you to open your mouth and swallow every demonic altar, witchcraft spell, subversive activity, ploy, plot and plan of the enemy to destroy my life and destiny in Jesus' name I pray.

Heavenly Father, I appeal to the judicial testimony of the blood of Jesus to wipe out every legal right and standing that the adversary had in the Courts of Heaven against my piece of real estate or that of my city or country, in Jesus' name. Heavenly Father, I give back everything of benefit that would cause the enemy to say, I have made you rich. I only want whatever comes from the presence of the Lord. Heavenly Father you said, "If my people who are called by name shall humble themselves, seek my face and forsake their wicked ways then I hear from heaven and heal their land." Heavenly Father, I ask for your forgiveness for the actions of our forefathers that defiled this land. Heavenly Father I ask that you grant me a righteous verdict concerning the land that the soil in my hand represents.

Earth, Earth…hear the words of my mouth and release the good of the land, favor, divine relationships, businesses, investments, employments, physical health and material prosperity into my life in accordance with the predetermined counsel of God for my life in Christ Jesus. Earth, Earth…hear the Word of the Lord. I decree and declare that my physical body will never return to the dust until my spirit has finished its divine assignment here on Earth, in Jesus' name I pray. I cancel and nullify the spirit of premature physical death in my life. I will live a long and healthy life, in Jesus' name.

Heavenly Father, I now speak to the Earth that makes up my physical or humus body and I say, "Earth, Earth…I command you to open your mouth and vomit every desire for unhealthy and toxic foods. I charge you in the mighty name of Jesus of Nazareth to embrace a new appetite for life-giving foods that glorify God and extend my physical life here on Earth. I decree and declare that as of this moment, my humus body will be overwhelmed by divine health, in Jesus' name I pray. I decree and declare that I receive God's supernatural healing of all the members and systems of my physical body of dirt. *Heavenly Father, I now make a motion and ask you to seal this proclamation and make it part of the official documents of the Courtroom of Heaven that Satan's kingdom cannot subvert, in the name of Jesus of Nazareth.* Heavenly Father, I also request your royal and supreme court to issue a divine restraining order against any territorial spirits that would like to visit upon me, what your Supreme Court has just delivered me from. May you assign high-ranking angelic officers of the Courts of Heaven to enforce this divine restraining order. In Jesus name. Amen!

**FINAL NOTE:** *After praying the above prayer, put the dirt (Earth) in your hand back into the soil as a prophetic statement that the Earth will now swallow all the diabolical plans of the devil against you. Start praising God in anticipation of the miracles He has just released in your life.*

# TESTIMONIALS

We used to have a lot of Cats that would invade our yard and make lots of noise at night. It was quite chilling. This went on for years unbated. Needless to say I did not look forward to sleeping at night. After I heard Dr. Myles teach on I speak to the Earth at Celebration Church in Zimbabwe, I appropriated the prayer and since then the Cats and the noise they were making disappeared. Hallelujah.

**Linda, Zimbabwe**

We live in Germany, Its been over year since Dr. Myles led us in a prayer to speak to the earth, we had a few situations where we were having some real difficulties, it had been about a year and half that we were fighting to get our own money from the IRS...the next day we made a call, it was suddenly taken care of. We got our tax money. It seems like it was in the area of finances, when we spoke to the Earth, I could sense that it was truly the difference we need, we had something happen with our student loans, there were demanding a payment that we couldn't pay...but after speaking to the Earth that changed immediately and we didn't have to pay a single penny. We are thankful for the word of God through the man of God, it has definitely changed our life.

**Jeff and Stacy, Germany**

## CHAPTER NINE

A Land Flowing With Milk & Honey
**By Rabbi Yuval Cherlow**

*https://www.myjewishlearning.com/article/a-land-flowing-with-milk-honey/*

# ABOUT AUTHOR

Dr. Francis Myles is the founder of Marketplace Bible International, a digital media company and Francis Myles International, an international apostolic ministry to the nations. He is also the senior pastor of Lovefest Church International, a thriving multiracial congregation based in Tempe, Arizona. He is also a life coach to "Movers and Shakers" in the Marketplace as well as government leaders. He is also the author of *The Order of Melchizedek* a book that has garnered worldwide acclaim. He has been featured on TBN's *Praise The Lord Program*, Daystar and God-TV networks. He has also been a special guest on Sid Roth's "Its Supernatural TV show." He is happily married to the love of his life Carmela Real Myles and they reside in the Phoenix Metropolis in Arizona.

New House w French Doors
Door in My bathroom to store room
Door in living room moved. Window
on My bedroom wall on North side
Shelves in Kitchen for books &
new place for Computer desk. Pantry
Closet for towels & sheets. Bathroom
tiled shower w room for Burke to
Move around w handles so we won't
fall in tub or shower. New tile
in whole house, New countert.
double glass windows. Stucko
on whole House. Fences? Need
Landscape - All new Appliance in
the house. Oct house is down so now
they and start Construction 10-16-18
the Old House burded down Jan 21, 20
Moved into new House Oct 24, 2019 - Not
Complete yet.

99300170R00067

Made in the USA
Columbia, SC
11 July 2018